Philosophy of Religion:
The Key Thinkers

Continuum *Key Thinkers*

The *Key Thinkers* series is aimed at undergraduate students and offers clear, concise and accessible edited guides to the key thinkers in each of the central topics in philosophy. Each book offers a comprehensive overview of the major thinkers who have contributed to the historical development of a key area of philosophy, providing a survey of their major works and the evolution of the central ideas in that area.

***Key Thinkers* in Philosophy forthcoming from Continuum:**

Aesthetics, Edited by Alessandro Giovannelli
Epistemology, Edited by Stephen Hetherington
Ethics, Edited by Tom Angier
Philosophy of Language, Edited by Barry Lee
Philosophy of Science, Edited by James Robert Brown

Philosophy of Religion: The Key Thinkers

Edited by
Jeffrey J. Jordan

continuum

Continuum International Publishing Group

The Tower Building
11 York Road
London SE1 7NX

80 Maiden Lane
Suite 704
New York, NY 10038

www.continuumbooks.com

British Library Cataloguing-in-Publication Data
A catalogue record for this book is available from the British Library.

ISBN: HB: 978-1-4411-0994-1
PB: 978-1-4411-9215-8

Library of Congress Cataloging-in-Publication Data
Philosophy of religion : the key thinkers / edited by Jeffrey J. Jordan.
    p. cm.
Includes index.
ISBN 978-1-4411-0994-1 – ISBN 978-1-4411-9215-8
1. Religion--Philosophy. 2. Christianity–Philosophy. I. Jordan, Jeff, 1959- II. Title.

BL51.P54535 2010
210–dc22

                                                                  2010021126

Typeset by Newgen Imaging Systems Pvt Ltd, Chennai, India
Printed and bound in India by Replika Press Pvt Ltd

Contents

Contents

Contributors

Peter Byrne is Emeritus Professor of Ethics and Philosophy of Religion, King's College London. He is the author of *Kant on God* (Ashgate, 2007) and seven other books in ethics and the philosophy of religion. He is editor of *Religious Studies: An International Journal for the Philosophy of Religion*.

Richard M. Gale is Professor Emeritus at the University of Pittsburgh and is the author of: *The Language of Time* (Routledge & Kegan Paul, 1968); *On the Nature and Existence of God* (Cambridge University Press, 1991); *The Divided Self of William James* (Cambridge University Press, 1999); and *John Dewey's Quest for Unity* (Prometheus Press, 2010)

William Hasker is Professor Emeritus of Philosophy at Huntington University. His books include *God, Time, and Knowledge* (Cornell 1989), *The Emergent Self* (Cornell 1999), and *The Triumph of God Over Evil* (InterVarsity 2008. He is a past editor of the journal *Faith and Philosophy*.

David Johnson is Associate Professor of Philosophy at Yeshiva University, and the author of two books: *Hume, Holism, and Miracles* (Cornell University Press, 1999) and *Truth without Paradox* (Rowman & Littlefield, 2004).

Jeff Jordan is Professor of Philosophy at the University of Delaware, and the author of *Pascal's Wager: Pragmatic arguments and belief in God* (Oxford University Press, 2006).

Graham Oppy is Professor of Philosophy at Monash University. His books include: *Ontological Arguments and Belief in God* (Cambridge University Press, 1996), *Philosophical Perspective on Infinity* (Cambridge

University Press, 2006), and *Arguing about Gods* (Cambridge University Press, 2006). He is Chairman of Council of the Australasian Association of Philosophy, and Head of the School of Philosophical, Historical and International Studies at Monash.

Katherin Rogers is a Professor in the Philosophy Department at the University of Delaware. She is the author of four books including, *Perfect Being Theology* (Edinburgh University Press, 2000) and *Anselm on Freedom* (Oxford University Press, 2008).

William L. Rowe is Professor Emeritus at Purdue University, and the author of five books, including *The Cosmological Argument* (Princeton University Press, 1975), *Thomas Reid on Freedom and Morality* (Cornell University Press, 1991), and *Is God Free?* (Oxford University Press, 2004). He is a past president, 1986–87, of the American Philosophical Association, Central Division.

Michael Tooley is a Distinguished College Professor in the Philosophy Department at the University of Colorado at Boulder, and the author or co-author of five books, including *Causation: A Realist Approach* (Oxford University Press, 1987), *Time, Tense, and Causation* (Oxford University Press, 1997) and, with Alvin Plantinga, *Knowledge of God* (Blackwell Publishing, 2008). He is a past president of the Australasian Association of Philosophy, 1983–1984, and president, 2010–2011, of the American Philosophical Association, Pacific Division.

Mark R. Wynn is Senior Lecturer in the Philosophy of Religion at the University of Exeter. He is the author of *God and Goodness* (Routledge, 1999), *Emotional Experience and Religious Understanding* (Cambridge University Press, 2005), and *Faith and Place* (Oxford University Press, 2009).

CHAPTER 1

KEY THINKERS IN THE PHILOSOPHY OF RELIGION: AN INTRODUCTION

Jeff Jordan

Inquiries into the existence and nature of God have been frequent in the history of Western philosophy, with nearly every famous philosopher having his say. Often these discussions are difficult today to understand, whether due to style and vocabulary differences from hundreds of years of change, or due to issues that do to lend themselves to a quick and easy read. The chapters which follow explore many of the important arguments for or against the existence of God produced by some of the most influential philosophers in western thought. And they do so with the aim of accurately capturing the reasoning of the philosophers in a way that makes that reasoning accessible today.

The first chapter features a debate between two theists over the nature of God. A fundamental question in the philosophy of religion concerns the meaning of the term 'God'. Professor Katherin Rogers arguments that the classical model of God found in thinkers such as Augustine and Thomas, and most pre-eminently in Anselm, is still today the model most appropriate for theistic belief and practice. Professor William Hasker argues that the classical model of God as an atemporal being who is omniscient and omnipotent does not adequately reflect the picture of God found in the Bible, and, moreover, the classical model is incompatible with significant human freedom. Rather than the classical or Anselmian view of God, Hasker suggests theists should accept what's known as the Open view of God.

The ontological argument developed by Anselm in the eleventh century is the topic of the Chapter 2. Anselm's ontological argument attempts to show that one cannot consistently hold both that God is that than which no greater can be conceived, and that God does not exist, since to hold both results in a contradiction. Professor Graham Oppy examines the reasoning of Anselm's argument, as well as several contemporary versions of the Ontological argument, and concludes that a careful scrutiny leads to serious doubts about either the logical structure of ontological arguments, or serious doubts about the independence of the premises from the conclusion, or serious doubts whether the conclusion in fact supports the existence of God.

The cosmological argument is the focus of Chapter 3, with William Rowe expositing the first two of Thomas Aquinas's famous 'five ways' of proving that God exists. Professor Rowe argues that both of Thomas's arguments suffer from several problems. One problem is that Thomas seems to assume that something can qualitatively change from one state (say, being cold) to another state (being hot) only if it is caused to do so by something that is already in the second state. But this assumption seems obviously wrong, since, for example, women are not made pregnant by pregnant women. Another problem is that Thomas provides no reason to exclude the possibility that something can occur simply as a brute fact. That something can come from nothing, in other words. A third problem Rowe mentions is that Thomas provides no clear reason why a series involving causes or change must terminate with a first cause. What precludes an infinite series of things causing other things? Rowe suggests that Thomas distinguishes between *per se* series and *accidental* series, with the former requiring a first member, while the latter may proceed to infinity.

The design argument is the topic of Chapter 5, especially the design argument formulated by William Paley. Paley's argument is too often dismissed as either having been pre-empted by David Hume's objections to the design argument published nearly 30 years prior to Paley, or rendered obsolete by Darwin, some 60 years later. Professor Mark Wynn in a careful study of Paley's argument shows that this common dismissal is wrong. Paley's argument has interest despite Hume and Darwin. Wynn shows that Paley's argument is not an argument from analogy, but is better understood as an Abductive argument, or an inference to the best explanation. As such it avoids Hume's objections to analogical arguments. Paley's argument may elude Darwinian objections as well with its appeal to considerations which are presupposed by Darwin's theory, but are not explained by it.

The moral argument is the focus of Chapter 6, and in particular the version of the moral argument presented by its most famous proponent, Immanuel Kant. Peter Byrne notes that moral arguments generally come in two kinds: evidential moral arguments, and non-evidential ones. The former kind involves arguing that some alleged fact about morality provides reason for thinking that God exists. Professor Byrne takes an evidential argument offered by Robert Adams, and explores how a non-theist might respond to the argument. During this exploration Professor Byrne notes a bootstrapping problem with any view that holds that normative obligation flows from divine commands: there will always be at least one alleged normative fact which cannot be explained by appealing to the principle that one ought always to obey God – where would the normativity accompanying that principle arise? Professor Byrne also vets Kant's non-evidential moral argument. Non-evidential arguments do not appeal to evidence, but contend rather that our commitment to moral rationality, for instance, commits us to the existence of God. Professor Byrne's main judgement concerning moral arguments of either kind is that such arguments involve contested issues – whether there are moral facts for instance – which leave the critic ample room to deny the force of the argument.

It is not uncommon that persons report having had experiences in which they take themselves to have had a direct but nonsensory perception of God. Such reports range from the dramatic extreme that might be termed 'mystical' to the more ordinary of one having the sense of being forgiven, or being called to this or that vocation. Might a theistic argument be erected upon a foundation of such reports? One of the great American philosophers, William James, pursued this question, especially in his 1902 masterpiece, *The Varieties of Religious Experience*. As Professor Richard Gale points out James is probably the first to develop a kind of argument that is often found among theistic thinkers today, an appeal to the strong similarities between ordinary sense perceptions and the reports of nonsensory perceptions offered by mystics. This kind of argument from analogy is found today, for instance, in works by the theistic philosophers William Alston, William Wainwright and Richard Swinburne. But, as Gale notes, James was not a classical theist, rejecting as he did the omnipotence of the divine, yet he was not a naturalistic or atheist either. James held that mystical experiences provided evidence that there was something more found in the universe than is discerned by the ordinary senses. If James is right then certain religious and mystical experiences are properly considered cognitive in nature – they provide informative about reality. They provide more than feelings, as some can be taken as evidence of the supernatural. Professor Gale's chapter provides an informative survey of William James's important work on religious experience.

The ontological argument as well as the cosmological, and the design arguments are all clear examples of theistic evidential arguments: arguments intended to provide good reason for believing that the proposition that God exists is more likely than not. Besides theistic evidential arguments, there are also theistic non-evidential arguments, including pragmatic arguments. Pragmatic arguments for theism are designed to motivate and support belief even in the absence of strong evidential support. These arguments seek to show that theistic belief is permissible, even if one does not think that it is likely that God exists. Pragmatic arguments employ prudential reasons on behalf of their conclusions. The most famous theistic pragmatic argument was offered by Blasé Pascal in the 1600s, his famous wager. In Chapter 8 I examine Pascal's wager by examining the four versions of the wager that Pascal formulated, the logic of those wagers, and I explore the two objections that are thought by most to present the most serious challenge to Pascalian wagering: the many-gods objection, and the evidentialist objection.

Several of the historical religions of the world – think of Judaism, for example, or Christianity – are purported cases of revealed religion. Religions that depend on an alleged divinely disclosed set of propositions (think of the Bible) or some kind of inspired teaching, and on certain events which are reported miracles (the deliverance out of Egypt, or the resurrection of Jesus, for example). A miracle, one might say, is an event that violates a law of nature. In his 1748 essay 'On Miracles', Chapter 10 of his *Enquiry Concerning Human Understanding*, David Hume argued that no rational person can accept testimony of miracles. If Hume is correct, then the superstructure of, say, Christianity would topple with the loss of its allegedly miraculous base – if the reports of Jesus' resurrection are a sham, so too would be any doctrines erected on those reports. Hume's essay has stirred controversy for over two hundred years, not just for its anti-religious implications but even regarding how to interpret Hume's reasoning. David Johnson, in Chapter 9, argues trenchantly that a common way of interpreting Hume in fact misinterprets Hume, and further, that Hume's essay lacks the support of any cogent argument. Johnson's foil is the philosopher Robert Fogelin, who championed the standard way of interpreting Hume in his 2003 book, *A Defense of Hume on Miracles* (Princeton University Press). Professor Johnson, then, has two targets in his sights: Hume and Professor Fogelin.

The strongest challenge to theistic belief is the problem of evil, which deals with the pain and suffering of innocent beings. As summarized by the character Philo in Part X of Hume's 1779 work, *Dialogues Concerning Natural Religion*, the problem of evil is:

> Is [God] willing to prevent evil, but not able? then is he impotent. Is he able, but not willing? then is he malevolent. Is he both able and willing? whence then is evil?

Like his attack on the credibility of miracle reports, Hume's formulation of the problem of evil is historically influential, and philosophically significant. Professor Michael Tooley provides a careful reading of Hume's development of the problem of evil in the *Dialogues Concerning Natural Evil*, and notes that Hume attempts to use the occurrence of evil to block any inference to the goodness of the cause or causes of the world, and as an argument contra the existence of God. Professor Tooley argues that Hume's formulation of the argument contra the existence of God, based on evil is significant in at least three ways. First, Hume, via the character of Philo, presents both an incompatibility version of the problem of evil, and an evidential version. An incompatible version argues that the occurrence of evil is logically incompatible with the existence of God; while an evidential version argues that evil, whether its variety, its quantity, or other facts about evil provides strong evidence against the existence of God. Second, Hume also focuses on concrete examples of evil, real cases of suffering, rather than treating suffering in the abstract. And third, Hume introduces discussion of four hypotheses regarding the origins of the universe – the cause or causes of the world are perfectly good, perfectly evil, a balance of good and evil, or are indifferent – and argues that experience of the amount and distribution of good and evil strongly supports the fourth hypothesis over the other three.

Philosophy of religion is a vibrant and lively area of philosophy, with much debate and innovative developments employing new methodologies to explore old questions. It is also an area of philosophy that extends well beyond the theoretical, to encompass some of the most pressing existential questions, including does God exist? Does suffering provide strong evidence that God does not exist? How should one conceive of God? And is it ever permissible to believe when lacking conclusive evidence? The essays that follow provide a guided tour along the historic paths which great thinkers in the past trod in trying to answer those questions.

CHAPTER 2

ANSELM AND THE CLASSICAL IDEA OF GOD: A DEBATE

Katherin Rogers & William Hasker

The classical view of God: Rogers

Before we proceed far in the philosophy of religion we should address the question of what we mean by the term 'God' and try to grasp, however haltingly, some understanding of the divine nature. Anselm of Canterbury speaks for the classical tradition of Christian philosophy which encompasses medieval philosophers like Augustine and Thomas Aquinas when, in his *Proslogion*, he defines God as 'that than which no greater can be conceived'.[1] He goes on in this work to attempt to prove the existence of God based on this definition and then to unpack the divine attributes in conformity with the definition. The present paper sketches Anselm's understanding of some of these attributes with an eye to disarming some contemporary criticisms.

But why adopt the *Proslogion* definition as our guiding principle when pondering the nature of God? Anselm believes that the Bible is the inerrant word of God and that the decisions of the Church Councils are guided by the Holy Spirit and so are absolutely trustworthy. Aren't these sufficient? In Anselm's view, reason can help us to further understand the Truth these sources deliver. And this is crucial for several reasons. One is expressed by Augustine's dictum that we cannot love what we do not know. The Christian is commanded to love God and the search for better understanding is also a journey towards a more profound love of God. The Christian is also commanded to love his neighbour.

While reasoned arguments can help the committed believer to better understand, they can also strengthen a faith that is weak, and bring the nonbeliever to belief. Anselm takes it that charity requires the philosopher to make the arguments which may help the neighbour.

But why insist on 'that than which no greater can be conceived'? Anselm himself simply assumes this as the correct definition and an appropriate starting point for philosophizing about God. In recent times, though, the Anselmian approach has been accused of presenting a God who is too remote, too 'hellenized', to be identified with the personal divinity of the Judeo-Christian tradition, and so it becomes important to defend the methodology. There are both religious and philosophical reasons for taking the *Proslogion* definition as a foundational and non-negotiable principle. On the religious side, the Judeo-Christian tradition holds that it is the very nature of God that He alone is worthy of worship. Lesser beings might rightly be esteemed or feared, but not worshipped. That is a unique response which may be directed only at God. Suppose now that you worship a being that you take to be a very great thing, perhaps the best thing in the universe, but than whom you *can* conceive of a greater. The powers of human conception are woefully limited. The being towards whom you direct your worship must be quite diminutive, if even your feeble powers are capable of conceiving of a greater. Is such a being really a proper object of worship? And worse, if you can conceive of a greater being – in fact, of a being than which no greater can be conceived – you cannot rule out the possibility that this greater being exists.[2] If this greater being exists, then *it* is the proper object of worship. It should be worshipped even by the lesser divinity to whom you have dedicated yourself. But in that case, the claim to being the appropriate object of worship is not a necessary trait of your lesser god. It might contingently happen to be the best thing in the universe, but it is not, by its very nature, worthy of worship. Only that than which no greater can be conceived can be, by nature, the uniquely appropriate object of worship and so only it can be the God of the Judeo-Christian tradition.

A second reason for beginning where Anselm begins is that, insofar as the Western tradition has marshalled philosophical reasons for belief in God in the form of arguments for His existence, many of these arguments point towards the existence of that than which no greater can be conceived. This is certainly true of the *Proslogion* argument, where the first premise is that this is the proper definition of God. (Someone might respond that Anselm's argument is so obviously unsound that it need not be taken into account, but almost no discussion of the 'ontological' argument understands it in Anselm's original version. To my knowledge, this version has not been shown to be unsound.[3]) And many of the causal arguments point to a being who, as the source of the universe, transcends the limitations inherent in it. If our already limited cognitive capabilities conceive of a divinity whom we recognize to be limited, it is likely that we are imposing on this conception the sort of limitations inherent in created being. But the God to Whom the arguments argue is a God who transcends all of that, so it seems apt to insist that He is that than which no greater can be conceived.

In saying that God is that than which no greater can be conceived, Anselm does not intend to suggest that the limited human intellect is indeed capable of fully comprehending God. We can speak and think correctly about God, and our terms and concepts apply univocally to God and creatures, and yet the reality of the divine nature transcends what we can really grasp. Anselm adopts the time-honoured Platonic analogy: Although we can see the sunlight, we are blinded if we try to gaze directly at the Sun.[4] In attempting, in however limited a way, to understand the nature of God, we must not confine our conception to what the human intellect can imagine or picture to itself. And, if we see that something must *be* the case, we should not reject it just because we cannot grasp *how* it must be the case.[5]

What, then, are the attributes of that than which no greater can be conceived? Let us start with the more obvious ones. Anselm holds God is perfectly powerful, perfectly knowledgeable, and perfectly good. But Anselm's classic conception of these traits differs significantly from that of many contemporary philosophers of religion. Divine omnipotence certainly does not mean that God can do anything logically possible for *someone* to do. It means that God can do anything logically possible for *a perfect and unlimited being* to do. God cannot make a rock too heavy for Him to lift.[6] Omnipotence also entails that God is the absolute source of all that is not Himself and that really exists. That last phrase has to be added lest someone suppose that God is the source of evil. In the classic tradition evil is not any sort of substance or object. It is the lack of what ought to be there.[7] Even the laws of logic and mathematics exist in dependence upon God as a reflection of the divine nature.[8] And God keeps all creation in being from moment to moment. What things *are* is what He thinks them to be, and if He were to stop thinking a thing, it would cease to be.[9] Regarding divine omniscience, God knows absolutely everything, including the future.[10] Regarding divine goodness, God's very nature is the standard for good, and all that is good or valuable is so through copying or reflecting the divine nature.[11]

Besides omnipotence, omniscience and perfect goodness, Anselm and the classic tradition defend other attributes less widely accepted today; simplicity, immutability and eternity. Anselm argues that, though triune, God is not composed of parts. A thing composed of parts is divisible, if only conceptually. But to be divided is to be destroyed. That than which no greater can be conceived cannot even be thought to be corruptible.[12] God's omnipotence, omniscience and goodness are not separate qualities. His nature *is* His act of doing all He does, which is identical with His act of knowing all He knows. And this act is the standard for value.[13] As simple, God cannot suffer change – no change at all! A thing which remains, while undergoing change, must be composite with an attribute which changes while the substrate does not.[14] But how could Anselm's God, the living God of the Judeo-Christian tradition, the God who makes the world and interacts with it moment by moment, *possibly* be immutable? Anselm, in fact, claims to show that God *had to* become incarnate. How could a God who actually enters into physical creation, changing human history in such a radical way, be immutable?

The question of the relationship between a changing world and an unchanging God was a perennial and vexed one in the Middle Ages. It motivated Augustine's famous meditation on time in *Confessions* 11.[15] It drove the debate between the Aristotelians and the more 'fundamentalist' Muslims which inspired a general distrust of philosophy in the Islamic world.[16] In order to solve the problem, Thomas Aquinas employs his extremely difficult point that, while creatures are really related to God, God is not really related to creatures; a view that can seem to isolate God from His creation.[17] Anselm, like other classical theists, holds that God is eternal, and proposes a theory of divine eternity which provides the metaphysical tools to solve the problem of an immutable God who is nonetheless an actor in His temporal creation. It all hinges on accepting the correct view of time.

Anselm is arguably the first philosopher in history to propound, in an explicit and conscious way, a four-dimensionalist or eternalist analysis of time.[18] (I prefer the former label because 'eternal' has traditionally been used to describe God's mode of being.) Four-dimensionalism is opposed to presentism. On a presentist theory of time, all that there is the present moment of time with all its contents. The past and future are absolutely non-existent. The four-dimensionalist view holds that all times and all their contents have equal ontological status. Past, present and future are indexed to the perspective of a given perceiver at a given point in time, rather like here and there are relative to a given perceiver at a given point in space. God is 'outside' of time in the sense that He does not exist as stretched out across the moments of time the way temporal creatures do. But He is not 'apart' from the temporal world. Rather all times and all they contain are immediately present to God, kept in being by His unified act of thinking.

Why does Anselm say this? The main alternative is presentism. All that exists is the present moment. That means that God exists only in the present moment, since that is all there is.[19] Anselm's starting point is the greatness of God, and so the questions are these: Which demonstrates greater power, to be able, at each moment, to act directly upon only that single moment of time and its contents, *or* to be able, in a single act, to act directly upon all times and all their contents? Surely the latter. Which demonstrates greater knowledge, to have an immediate cognition only of the present moment, such that you remember the past, and, if you know the future, know it indirectly from things in the present, *or* to 'see' all events at all times directly? Knowing directly is a better way of knowing than knowing indirectly.[20] And more knowledge is greater than less. Four-dimensionalism allows us to conceive of a God who directly knows what is to us the past, present and future. If we hold that God knows only the present and the past, we have abandoned the claim that God is that than which no greater can be conceived.

What if we insist that God, in His perfect goodness, has made creatures with libertarian free will, and that free will and divine fore-knowledge are incompatible? Anselm is the first Christian philosopher, and perhaps the first philosopher ever, to offer a systematic and metaphysically sophisticated analysis of libertarian freedom.[21] Anselm holds that the created agent must have open options. The agent experiences competing motivations, and it is absolutely not determined which motivation will win out. His free choices arise from his own will.[22] If we do not insist upon this robust free will then we would have to say that, ultimately, God is the cause of sin. And that, says Anselm, is logically impossible, since to sin is to will what God wills that you not will. Period.[23] But if God knows today what you will choose x tomorrow, then, when tomorrow comes, you cannot do other than God knew today you would do, and so you do not have open options – or so it seems.

On Anselm's four-dimensionalist analysis, since it is all 'now' to God, it is your choosing x tomorrow that grounds God's knowledge today that you choose x tomorrow. True, you cannot do other than choose x tomorrow, but that is because you choose x tomorrow. The lack of options is the same as that involved in saying that, if you are reading this *now*, God knows that you are reading this now, and so you cannot be doing other than reading this now. But does that show that you are not reading freely? The open options required for libertarian freedom surely need not include the option to do, at a given time, other than one does at that time, since that would be logically impossible.[24] Thus four-dimensionalism allows Anselm to reconcile freedom with divine foreknowledge.

Are there reasons to reject four-dimensionalism? Some have said that it denies change in the created world, but so long as change means things being different from one time to another, four-dimensionalism is compatible with change. Some have said that four-dimensionalism conflicts with our ordinary experience. But no theory of time seems a comfortable fit with experience. For example, presentism holds that all that exists is the present moment, the unextended point at which the non-existent future becomes the non-existent past. Is that how things seem? More importantly, even if four-dimensionalism were more distant from ordinary experience than other theories, God's perfection is non-negotiable and trumps human experience. Adopting four-dimensionalism allows Anselm to reconcile freedom with divine foreknowledge and divine agency with divine immutability. It also allows him to defend the most robust conception of divine greatness, including the most extensive possible divine power and knowledge. Perhaps four-dimensionalism seems counter-intuitive, but that God might be that than which we *can* conceive a greater is impossible. Better to adopt the difficult theory of time than to abandon Anselm's God!

A non-classical alternative to Anselm: William Hasker

My role in this discussion is to offer a non-classical alternative to Anselm's classical theism, as presented by Professor Rogers. In spite of the venerable tradition supporting the Anselmian view, not to mention its undeniable metaphysical elegance, I believe there is an alternative view which is superior both in its internal consistency and in its faithfulness to Scripture and Christian experience. I begin by setting out some of my disagreements with Anselm/Rogers,[25] and then present briefly the main lines of the alternative, non-classical option.

I am very happy, however, to express my agreement with much of what Rogers says early on in her piece. I agree that the Anselmian conception of God as 'that than which no greater can be conceived' needs to be fundamental for our reflections on God's nature. This is so, because only such an unsurpassably great being can be worthy of the absolute, unqualified love, worship and obedience that is demanded of us. And I also agree emphatically about the need for Christian philosophers and theologians to rigorously think through questions concerning the nature of God, so as to enable us to understand better (though still no doubt very inadequately) the One whom we love and worship.

Ironically, one major disagreement with Anselm/Rogers concerns what I take to be their over-confidence in human reason as it carries out this needed task of reflection. I call this ironic, because one would not usually expect a modern philosopher to chide a medieval theologian for being excessively rational! But I believe that Anselm and Rogers are far too optimistic about our ability to determine easily, almost by inspection, which attributes are fittingly ascribed to a God who is the greatest conceivable being. Rogers proceeds too quickly in concluding that, if we adopt certain conceptions of God's knowledge, 'we have abandoned the claim that God is that than which no greater can be conceived'. Before such conclusions can be warranted we need to have carefully scrutinized alternative views of the divine attributes for their internal logical consistency as well as their harmony or disharmony with all of the other things that need to be said about God. It is, unfortunately, all too easy for us to think up supposedly 'great-making' attributes which turn out to be either incoherent or in conflict with other things that need to be said about God.[26] I also believe that Scripture needs to play a larger role in our understanding of the divine attributes than it is able to do in the Anselmian way of proceeding. Some of these 'great-making' attributes are exceedingly difficult to reconcile with the Biblical picture of God.

Our substantive disagreements begin with the 'less widely accepted' attributes of simplicity, immutability and (timeless) eternity. About simplicity I have little to say, since those who defend the doctrine can't seem to agree on exactly what it means. To be sure, God is not assembled out of parts; that much is agreed upon by all. The doctrine of divine simplicity, however, is supposed to mean a great deal more than this, but what that 'more' is remains in contention, so it is best to refrain from criticizing until there is a clear target for the criticism.

We turn next to a classical attribute not mentioned by Rogers, divine *impassibility*, which asserts that God cannot be affected by any negative emotion whatsoever. Anselm is quite explicit about this:

> So how, Lord, are you both merciful and not merciful? Is it not because you are merciful in relation to us but not in relation to yourself? You are indeed merciful according to what we feel, but not according to what you feel. For when you look with favor upon us in our sorrow, we feel the effect [*effectum*] of mercy, but you do not feel the emotion [*affectum*] of mercy. So you are merciful, because you save the sorrowful and spare those who sin against you, but you are also not merciful because you are not afflicted with any feeling of compassion for sorrow (*Proslogion* 8).[27]

Nicely stated, to be sure, but I submit that this 'lack of affect' is not at all what most of us would expect of a being who is said to be perfectly loving! And it is also difficult to reconcile with the Scriptures, according to which 'As a father has compassion for his children, so the LORD has compassion for those who fear him' (Psalm 103: 13).[28]

My main attention, however, will be focused on two other attributes: absolute immutability and divine timeless eternity. I agree that if God is to be absolutely immutable, God must be timeless. Otherwise, if God is temporal, there must be at least minimal changes in God, so that God's knowledge can match the changes that occur in the world. I also agree with Rogers that the view of God as timeless requires that we accept a four-dimensionalist view of time. If there is an objective, ever-changing temporal 'now', then there will be temporal facts – facts about what events have transpired up until the present moment – which a timeless God cannot know. For example, the events celebrated in the liturgy: 'Christ *has* died, Christ *has* risen, Christ *will* come again'.

Now, it is by no means clear that Anselm was a consistent four-dimensionalist in his view of time: as Rogers acknowledges, scholarly opinion is divided on this.[29] But let's suppose that she is right about Anselm's view, and consider the merits and demerits of that view. To begin with, it's not at all obvious that such a view is compatible with Scripture, which portrays throughout a 'living God . . . who makes the world and interacts with it moment by moment'.[30] There is quite a gap between the dynamically active God portrayed in Scripture and the timeless God of classical theism; that's why this was a 'perennial and vexed' question throughout the Middle Ages. Classical theists do not, of course, deny these Scriptural depictions of God; rather they develop elaborate theories, four-dimensionalism among them, showing how the two apparently conflicting conceptions of God can be reconciled. In the biblical stories, Calvin says, God 'lisps' to us – that is, talks baby-talk – as an accommodation to our limited understanding. But this raises a number of questions, these two among them: Just how did Calvin – or, for that matter, Anselm – get to be the 'adults' who are able to comprehend the 'deep truths' about God that apparently could not be revealed to the apostles and prophets? And why should we trust the philosophical sources of classical theism (among which Neoplatonism is prominent, as Rogers says) to be more accurate in their depiction of God than the Bible is?

The most important objection, however, is that divine timelessness and four-dimensionalism are inconsistent with the libertarian free will that it is essential, according to Anselm and Rogers, to attribute to human beings. According to Anselm/Rogers, free will requires that there be, for the agent, *alternative possibilities* at the time when she makes her choice.[31] That is to say, at the moment when she chooses it must be *really possible,* all things considered, for her to make a different choice than the one she actually makes. Now consider Annie, an agent who is in the process of making a libertarian choice between X and Y. Suppose she in fact chooses Y; this means that Annie's choice of Y exists eternally as part of the four-dimensional continuum. But in order for her choice to be free it must have been really possible, and really within Annie's power, to choose X instead of Y. And of course, her choice of X would bring about that it is her choice of X rather than her choice of Y that eternally exists as part of the continuum. But this means that, at the time when Annie makes her choice, *'there are future actions of [Annie's] which timelessly exist in the divine eternity which are such that it is in [Annie's] power, now, to bring about that those actions do not exist in eternity'.* In her book on Anselm, Rogers quotes the italicized sentence from an earlier article of my own, and responds, 'Of course this condition cannot be met'.[32] I certainly agree that it cannot – but, *pace* Rogers, what this shows is that the Anselm/Rogers view does not, as they both claim, make it possible for libertarian free will to coexist with the presence of all future events in God's eternity.

But now, what is the alternative to Anselmian classical theism? The position taken here is that of 'open theism' or the 'openness of God', so called because it first came to prominence through the publication of a book by that name.[33] This is a version of orthodox Christian theism, according to which God is perfect in wisdom, goodness and power, and is the unique, self-sufficient creator of the universe, including all concrete entities other than God. God exists eternally as the Trinity of Father, Son and Holy Spirit; God the Son became a human being as Jesus of Nazareth, and as such lived a human life, died and rose again from the dead for the salvation of humankind. Open theism, however, is not merely generic theism, not even generic Christian theism. Open theism has distinctive implications concerning the nature of God, and God's relationships with the world and with humankind, that distinguish it from other versions of theism. The central idea of open theism is that God is 'open', that is, affected by and responsive to the world God has made, and especially to free and rational creatures such as human beings. In contrast with Aristotle's Unmoved Mover, the God of open theism has been characterized by Clark Pinnock as the 'Most Moved Mover'; God is more deeply affected by what occurs in his creation than we can ever imagine. Also included is the idea that God is open to the future, which is itself open, indeterminate in many respects and waiting to be determined both by God and by human beings.

In several ways open theism is sharply distinguished from Anselmian classical theism. However, open theism agrees with Anselm in the insistence

Anselm and the Classical Idea of God: A Debate

17

that God is supremely perfect in power, knowledge and goodness. (The issue is not *whether* God is perfect, but rather in what this perfection consists.) God is temporal, not timeless; God's eternity does not mean that temporal categories are inapplicable to God, but rather that God is *everlasting*: unlike the creatures, God always has existed and always will exist. Time is not an alien medium within which God is 'trapped' or 'limited'; rather time, in the sense of a changeful succession of states, is inherent in God's own nature. God is unchanging in his nature and character; his wisdom, power and faithfulness to us never alter in the slightest degree. But God's experience does vary from time to time, as indeed it must if he is to be aware of what occurs and changes in the world, and if God is to respond to the creatures in the way the Bible and Christian tradition insist that he does. One of the most profound differences between open theism and classical theism concerns the doctrine of divine impassibility. Open theism insists that God, far from being impassible, is deeply affected by events in the lives of his creatures: he suffers with us when we are afflicted, and rejoices when we find true happiness. To be sure, God is not controlled or overpowered by emotion in the way that often happens to us; rather God has chosen to sympathize with us, to share our joys and sorrows. For Christians, the supreme instance of this is the incarnation of God in Jesus Christ, but open theists insist that God's 'openness' to sharing our experiences is not limited to this; rather, God's presence in Jesus is a revelation of what God in his essential nature truly is, and thinks, and feels.

Open theists recognize God as having the power that would enable him to exert his rule over the world by unilaterally controlling everything that takes place. They believe, however, that God has not chosen to do this, but has instead bestowed upon his creatures a genuine power to make decisions of their own, including decisions as to whether or not to cooperate with God's loving purposes towards them. (In this, to be sure, open theism agrees with the Anselmian view, and we salute Anselm/Rogers for insisting on genuine freedom for the creatures, in opposition to Augustine, Calvin and many other proponents of classical theism.) This creates a real possibility of tragedy in the world, as our actual history illustrates all too vividly, but also makes possible a genuine, spontaneous response of love towards God that would be precluded were we merely, so to speak, puppets dancing on the ends of the divinely manipulated strings.

One final position taken by open theists is at once the most clearly distinctive feature of their view and the most controversial. Open theism holds that creatures are 'free' in the libertarian sense, meaning that it is really possible, in a given situation, for the creature to do something different than the thing it actually does.[34] Furthermore, the choices of this sort that will be made in the future *do not now exist,* and as such are unknowable for any being, God included. It is not a matter of God's knowledge being less than perfect; rather, with regard to these undetermined future events, there is simply nothing for God to know. Open theists argue that the lack of this sort of knowledge does not impede God in his providential governance of the world, though it does lead us to understand that governance in a different way than is typical of classical theism.[35]

This, then, is the non-classical alternative that is offered for your consideration. I bring these remarks to a close here, to leave space for the discussion as Professor Rogers and I continue to explore both our differences and our points of agreement.

An Anselmian response: Rogers

Thanks again to Professor Hasker. Anselm takes God to be the primary 'biblical writer', and so would hesitate to limit what might have 'been in the minds of the biblical authors'. He insists that God is *both* 'a timeless, utterly immutable God and a God who [from our perspective] lives and acts in time, and responds [with love] to what transpires in the world[.]' True, He does not change His mind. It is simply better not to make mistakes. On Hasker's reading the biblical God is just not 'that than which no greater can be conceived'.

And He knows future free choices. At t-1 Annie has the power to do both X and Y at t in the sense that her choice is not determined. Her choice alone decides whether she does X or Y and so produces the contents of the divine knowledge at t-1. If she chooses X then God knows she chooses X. Similarly if she chooses Y. This seems a robust enough sense of alternatives being 'in her power' to allow libertarian freedom and yet to admit of divine foreknowledge and a God than Whom no greater can be conceived.

A non-classical response: Hasker

If Annie's choice of Y exists timelessly as part of the four-dimensional continuum – or, alternatively, if God has always known that Annie chooses Y – then at the time when she chooses it is impossible that she will choose X instead of Y. But what it is impossible that a person should do is not in her power to do, so her choosing X is not an 'alternative possibility'. And causal indeterminacy by itself is not enough for free will.

There is no evidence that any of the biblical writers (including God, for that matter!) thought of God as timeless, and plenty of evidence that God responds to his creatures sometimes with sorrow and sometimes with anger – but yes, always with love. So in these respects, Anselm's view of God deviates from what we find in the Bible.

Yet in spite of these disagreements Anselm, Professor Rogers and I share a common faith and hope in a God who is incomparably greater than all we can say about him.

Notes

1 *Proslogion*, 2.
2 This may seem a little hasty. You might believe that the fact of evil shows the existence of Anselm's God to be impossible, while leaving open the possibility of the existence of lesser divinities. The classical tradition has laboured long, hard and, in my view, successfully, to respond to this point.
3 I try to situate the *Proslogion* argument within Anselm's Neoplatonic thought in Chapter 6 of *The Neoplatonic Metaphysics and Epistemology of Anselm of Canterbury* (Lewiston, NY: The Edwin Mellen Press, 1997).
4 See *Response to Gaunilo* 1, and *Proslogion* 14. See also Chapter 5 of *Neoplatonic Metaphysics*.
5 See *Why God Became Man* Book 1, 25. God cannot be or do anything logically impossible, and so there is some constraint on what we may attribute to God, but this is not a limitation on the divine nature, since the impossible is not really a thing to be or do.
6 *Proslogion* 7.
7 Nowadays evil is often identified with undeserved suffering. The classic tradition understands most human pain as the consequence of sin, and animal pain as an inevitable part of the causal system of nature which, in itself, is so valuable as to justify the pain. Real evil – what absolutely ought not be – is the privation or

corruption or destruction of some good, and/or the choice for the lesser and lower over what ought to be chosen.

8   Many contemporary philosophers of religion hold that there are abstracta of various sorts – necessary truths, for example – that exist independently of God. The classic tradition denies this.

9   See Anselm's *Monologion* 13–14. See also Chapter 7 of my *Perfect Being Theology* (Edinburgh: Edinburgh University Press, 2000), hereafter *PBT*.

10 See Anselm's *On the Harmony of God's Foreknowledge, Predestination, and Grace with Human Freedom* Book 1. See also *PBT* 6.

11 *Monologion*, 1–2. See also *PBT* 9.

12 *Proslogion*, 18.

13 *Monologion*, 17. See also *PBT* 3.

14 *Monologion*, 25. See also *PBT* 4.

15 See my *Anselm on Freedom* (Oxford: Oxford University Press, 2008), 165–6.

16 See my 'Anselm and His Islamic Contemporaries on Divine Necessity and Eternity,' *American Catholic Philosophical Quarterly* 81 (2007), 373–93.

17 *Summa Theologiae*, Ia. q.13, a. 7.

18 *Anselm on Freedom*, 176–84.

19 Brian Leftow argues that Anselm is a presentist, believing in a temporal *and* an eternal present, in 'Anselmian Presentism', *Faith and Philosophy* (forthcoming). I respond in 'Back to Eternalism', *Faith and Philosophy* (forthcoming in the same volume).

20 William Alston, 'Does God Have Beliefs?', *Religious Studies* 22 (1987), 287–306.

21 This is the overall theme of *Anselm on Freedom*.

22 See Anselm's *On the Fall of the Devil*, especially Chapters 13–14, and 27. See also *Anselm on Freedom* 73–8.

23 See Anselm's *On Free Will*, Chapter 8. See also *Anselm on Freedom* 88–92.

24 *Anselm on Freedom* 169–76; see also my 'The Necessity of the Present and Anselm's Eternalist Response to the Problem of Theological Fatalism', *Religious Studies* 43 (2007), 25–47. Classical theists such as Augustine and Aquinas would worry that this entails that creatures have an effect upon God. Anselm takes that consequence as a necessary part of the system in which God has made free beings.

25 For present purposes it will be both convenient and appropriate to treat Anselm and Rogers as a single unit. There may be some points at which Rogers disagrees with Anselm, but they will not come into play in this discussion.

26 Rogers herself supplies an example of this, when she points out that classical theists such as Anselm and Aquinas would object to the idea that creatures can have an effect on God. I agree with Anselm/Rogers that our idea of God must allow for libertarian free will for creatures (lest God be said to be the author of sin), and that libertarianism, in turn, requires that creatures should have an effect on God. But this provides a clear example of an allegedly 'great-making'

attribute – that of the absolute, comprehensive independence of God from creatures – that upon further reflection it is better *not* to ascribe to God.

27 *Anselm: Basic Writings,* trans. and ed. Thomas Williams (Indianapolis, Hackett Publishing Co., 2007), 85.

28 For an even more powerful evocation of the divine pathos, see Hosea, Chapter 2.

29 For reasons why Anselm may not be a four-dimensionalist, see my review of Rogers' *Anselm on Freedom* in *Religious Studies* 45/4 (2009), 499–504.

30 In the past a few biblical texts have been interpreted as supporting the doctrine of timeless eternity, but it has become clear that the view is read into the texts rather than derived from them. For discussion see Alan G. Padgett, *God, Eternity and the Nature of Time* (New York: St. Martin's Press, 1992), Chapter 2.

31 The need for alternative possibilities is sometimes denied, on account of the 'Frankfurt counterexamples' that allegedly depict situations in which persons are free and responsible in spite of the lack of alternative possibilities. I do not believe the Frankfurt cases are successful, but it is not necessary to argue this here, since Anselm/Rogers agree on the need for alternatives.

32 *Anselm on Freedom,* 171. The quoted sentence is from 'The Absence of a Timeless God,' in Greg Ganssle and David Woodruff, eds., *God and Time,* (Oxford: Oxford University Press, 2002), 198.

33 For open theism see Clark Pinnock, Richard Rice, John Sanders, William Hasker and David Basinger, *The Openness of God: A Biblical Challenge to the Traditional Understanding of God* (Downers Grove: InterVarsity Press, 1994). The theological implications of open theism are further developed in John Sanders, *The God Who Risks: A Theology of Providence* (Downers Grove: InterVarsity Press, 1998), and Clark H. Pinnock, *Most Moved Mover: A Theology of God's Openness* (Carlisle: Paternoster Press, 2001). For a sustained argument in favour of the view of God's knowledge affirmed by open theism see William Hasker, *God Time, and Knowledge* (Ithaca: Cornell University Press, 1989).

34 But not, of course, in *all* situations. Sensible libertarians recognize that there are a great many limitations and obstructions to human action that prevent us from being entirely free.

35 However, the view of God held by classical theists such as Anselm, who combine libertarian free will with divine timeless knowledge of all events, allows God *exactly the same resources* for his providential governance as does open theism. For argument, see *God, Time, and Knowledge,* Chapter 3.

CHAPTER 3

ANSELM AND THE ONTOLOGICAL ARGUMENT

Graham Oppy

St. Anselm (*ca.* 1033–1109) is widely regarded as the father of scholastic philosophy. From 1093, Anselm was Archbishop of Canterbury, though he spent much time in exile as a consequence of disputes with secular rulers. While he conducted a range of linguistic and analytical investigations, Anselm is perhaps best known for his proof of the existence and nature of God in the *Proslogion*, a work that appeared in 1078, at the time that he was prior of the Benedictine Abbey of Bec in Normandy.

There is disagreement about the structure and purpose of the *Proslogion*. I think that Anselm attempts to prove the existence of 'that than which no greater can be conceived' in Chapter 2, and then, in Chapter 3, tries to show that 'that than which no greater can be conceived' cannot even be conceived not to exist. In subsequent chapters, Anselm goes on to attempt to demonstrate a further range of attributes of 'that than which no greater can be conceived'. On this account, Chapter 2 contains the proof of the existence of a being that one might suspect is God; the rest of the work establishes that the being whose existence is established in Chapter 2 is, indeed, God.

Some interpreters claim that there is an independent argument for the existence of God in Chapter 3; other interpreters claim that there is a single argument for the existence of God that is contained in Chapters 2 and 3 together. (Some interpreters even claim that Anselm did not put forward any attempted proofs of the existence of God in the *Proslogion*.) One part of the explanation for this diversity in interpretative opinion is that it is clear that the arguments of Chapters 2 and Chapter 3 of the *Proslogion* have a formal similarity. In Chapter 2, Anselm argues that the assumption *that 'that than which no greater can be conceived' does not exist (in reality)* entails absurdities – whence we can conclude that 'that than which no greater can be conceived' does exist (in reality). In Chapter 3, Anselm argues that the assumption *that 'than than which no greater can be conceived' can be conceived not to exist (in reality)* entails absurdities – whence we can conclude that 'that than which no greater can be conceived' cannot be conceived not to exist. However, one might think that it is at least *prima facie* plausible to suppose that, if 'that than which no greater can be conceived' cannot be conceived not to exist, then 'that than which no greater can be conceived' exists. And, if one does think that, then one will think that the argument in Chapter 3 could also have been used as an independent route to the conclusion of the argument in Chapter 2. (If Anselm thought that there was a good argument from the claim *that 'that than which no greater can be conceived' cannot be conceived not to exist* to the claim *that 'that than which no greater can be conceived' exists*, he certainly does not set out that argument in the *Proslogion*. I take it that this fact provides significant support for my preferred interpretation of the structure and purpose of the *Proslogion*.)

The key passage in Chapter 2 of the *Proslogion* may be translated as follows (Mann (1972: 260–1), with some minor alterations):

> Thus even the fool is convinced that that than which no greater can be conceived is in the understanding, since when he hears this, he understands it; and whatever is understood is in the understanding. And certainly that than which no greater can be conceived cannot be in the understanding alone. For if it is even in the understanding alone, it can be conceived to exist in reality also, which is greater. Thus if that than which no greater can be conceived is in the understanding, then that than which no greater can be conceived is itself that than which a greater can be conceived. But surely this cannot be. Thus without doubt that than which a greater cannot be conceived exists, both in the understanding and in reality.

The argument in this passage has two major parts. In the first part, Anselm seems to argue in the following way:

1. When the fool hears the words 'that than which no greater can be conceived', he understands those words (Premise).

2. For any expression 'E', if 'E' is understood, then E exists in the understanding (Premise).
3. Hence, that than which no greater can be conceived exists in the understanding (Conclusion).

As it stands, there seems to be some slippage in this argument between talk of 'the understanding of the fool' and 'the understanding' (perhaps, say, 'the generic understanding of humanity'). While this slippage could be resolved in either of two ways, most interpreters choose to resolve this slippage in favour of talk of 'the understanding'. Adopting this resolution, we can recast the argument as follows:

1. The words 'that than which no greater can be conceived' are understood (Premise).
2. For any expression 'E', if 'E' is understood, then E exists in the understanding (Premise).
3. Hence, that than which no greater can be conceived exists in the understanding (From 1, 2).

While it seems clear – assuming uniform interpretation of key expressions in the premises and conclusion – that the conclusion of this argument is a logical consequence of the premises, there are various questions that can be asked about the premises. On the one hand, there are questions to be asked about the range of expressions for which it is even *prima facie* plausible to suppose that Premise 2 is true. And, on the other hand, there are questions to be asked about the nature of the theory that is implicit in serious talk about 'existence in the understanding'.

If we consider substitution instances of the schema 'E exists in the understanding', then we see that we only get meaningful outcomes if we restrict substitution instances of 'E' to something like referring terms: names, definite descriptions, quantifier phrases and the like:

a. Santa Claus exists in the understanding.
b. The tallest Martian exists in the understanding.
c. A man than whom none is greater exists in the understanding.
d. Tailless dragons exist in the understanding.

Other kinds of substitution instances for 'E' fail even to yield grammatically well-formed sentences:

a. Snow is white exists in the understanding.
b. Because exists in the understanding.
c. False exists in the understanding.
d. In the corner exists in the understanding.

However, while failure of this test is surely sufficient to rule out certain kinds of substitution instances, it is not clear whether passing this test suffices to establish that given substitution instances are acceptable: whether or not this is so will depend upon the further details of the account of what it is for something to exist in the understanding.

There are two related questions that arise in connection with Anselm's talk of 'understanding' and 'existence in the understanding'. On the one hand, there are questions about what kind of understanding of an expression 'E' suffices to make it the case that E exists in the understanding. And, on the other hand, there are questions about the development of a theoretical framework that will support talk of 'existence in the understanding'.

Can an expression 'E' be understood even if that expression is demonstrably self-contradictory – 'the non-square square' – or demonstrably necessarily uninstantiated – 'the greatest prime number' – or merely necessarily uninstantiated – 'the actual tallest inhabitant of the planet Mars'?

If we suppose that the answer to this question is 'No!', then it is not uncontroversial that Premise 1 of Anselm's argument is true: if it is necessarily the case that the expression 'that than which no greater can be conceived' is uninstantiated, then neither the fool nor anyone else understands that expression (in the relevant sense). On the plausible assumption that, if the expression 'that than which no greater can be conceived' is uninstantiated, then it is necessarily uninstantiated, it turns out that anyone who supposes that the expression 'that than which no greater can be conceived' is uninstantiated will be required to say that the expression 'that than which no greater can be conceived' cannot be understood in this relevant sense. Consequently, it will *not* turn out that 'even the fool is convinced that that than which no greater can be conceived is in the understanding'. While Anselm might still insist that the fool is wrong about this – because the expression 'that than which no greater can be conceived' is not uninstantiated – it seems that the upshot is nonetheless that Anselm's *argument* turns out to be question-begging: justified acceptance of Premise 1 presupposes justified acceptance of the conclusion of the argument.

If, on the other hand, we suppose that expressions that are demonstrably self-contradictory, or demonstrably necessarily uninstantiated, or otherwise necessarily uninstantiated can nonetheless be understood, then, given Premise 2, we shall be committed to the claim that there are things in the understanding that have self-contradictory, or necessarily jointly uninstantiable, properties in the understanding. Whether this is problematic will then depend upon the further details of our theory of existence and property instantiation in the understanding.

At least in rough outline, it might seem *prima facie* plausible to suppose that the following claims are implicit in Anselm's talk of 'existence in the understanding':

1. There are two domains of objects: reality and the understanding.
2. Some objects belong to exactly one of these domains.
3. Some objects belong to both of these domains.
4. There are no objects that belong to neither domain.
5. Objects that belong to reality do not have logically inconsistent properties, and nor do they suffer from logical incompleteness: in particular, for any pair of a property and the negation of that property, an object that belongs to reality has exactly one of the members of that pair of properties.
6. Objects that belong both to reality and the understanding may have different properties in reality and in the understanding: in particular, objects that belong to the understanding may – for all that has been said so far – have logically inconsistent properties or suffer from logical incompleteness in the understanding.
7. Given that objects that belong both to reality and the understanding may have different properties in reality and in the understanding, it cannot be that it is always sameness of properties that underwrites the *identity* of objects in reality with objects in the understanding (in those cases in which there is one object that exists in both domains).

But even this modest initial round of assumptions leads to serious trouble. If we suppose that an object exists in reality, then, on the assumption that that there are different guises under which that object can enter the understanding, it seems that we shall end up being committed to the view that *it* – the object that exists in reality – is *identical* to many different objects that exist in the understanding. That can't be right! Perhaps we might try saying that it is only *in the understanding* that these objects are distinct, but that also seems unsatisfying, not least because it seems pretty clear that we must be supposing that these objects can be distinguished from the theoretical standpoint from which we are elaborating the Anselmian theory.

As an alternative to the above attempt, we might try saying that objects that exist both in the understanding and in reality have *the very same* properties in the understanding that they have in reality. However, if we suppose that the properties that objects that exist in reality have in the understanding are thus radically independent of the way that we conceive of those object – we can, after all, be massively mistaken in our beliefs about the properties that are in fact possessed by objects that exist in reality – then we might also suppose that we actually have good reason to deny that there can be things in the understanding that have self-contradictory – or necessarily jointly uninstantiable – properties. For how could it be that the understanding is perfectly impervious to false conceptions of actually existing objects, and yet at the same time a sucker for incoherent conceptions of objects that do not actually exist?

I take it that the upshot of the discussion to this point is that it is highly doubtful whether anyone should accept Anselm's claim that *that than which no greater can be conceived* exists in the understanding. At the very least, pending a carefully developed account of existence in the understanding, it seems that the fool is certainly within his rights to refuse to accept the claim that *that than which no greater can be conceived* exists in the understanding, and that is enough to allow the fool to reject Anselm's argument with a clear conscience, and to ensure that Anselm should be able to see that his argument does not show that the fool is irrational on account of his rejection of the existence of *that than which no greater can be conceived*.

Given the nature of the difficulties that we have explored to this point, one might suspect that there will be difficulties in proceeding to examine the rest of Anselm's argument under the pretence that we can accept the claim that *that than which no greater can be conceived* exists in the understanding. Nonetheless, that is what we shall now try to do. On a straightforward reading, the second major part of Anselm's argument seems to run as follows:

1. If *that than which no greater can be conceived* exists in the understanding, then *that than which no greater can be conceived* can be conceived to exist in reality (Premise).
2. If *that than which no greater can be conceived* exists in reality then *it* is greater than *it* would be if *it* were to exist only in the understanding (Premise).
3. Hence, if *that than which no greater can be conceived* exists only in the understanding, then it is something than which a greater can be conceived (From 1, 2).
4. *That than which no greater can be conceived* is not something than which a greater can be conceived (Premise).
5. Hence, *that than which no greater can be conceived* does not exist only in the understanding (From 4, 5).

One question that arises immediately concerns the relationship between (a) conceiving objects to possess certain properties and (b) possession of properties by those objects in the understanding. There are two distinct claims here that merit consideration. First, it might be that, when an object is conceived to possess a property, then the object possesses that property in the understanding. Second, it might be that, when an object possesses a property in the understanding, that object is conceived to possess that property. Since these claims are independent, there are four different relationships that might hold between conceiving objects to possess properties and possession of properties by objects in the understanding: exactly one of the distinct claims is true, or both are true, or neither is true.

To further complicate matters, it might be that the claims mentioned at the end of the preceding paragraph hold for all but a distinguished class of properties, rather than for all properties. So, for example, it might be that, while something that is conceived to be red has the property of being red in the understanding, something that is conceived to exist in reality does not have the property of existing in reality in the understanding, because existence in reality is one of the distinguished class of properties for which it fails to be true that, if an object is conceived to possess a property, then the object possesses that property in the understanding. Since it is plausible to suppose that, if there is a distinguished class of properties for which the claims in question fail to hold, then *existence in the understanding* and *existence in reality* will be among those properties, a proper investigation of Anselm's argument really needs to consider at least eight different relationships that might hold between conceiving objects to possess properties and possession of properties by objects in the understanding.

Now, of course, if we suppose that, in the case of objects that exist in reality, the properties that those objects possess in the understanding are radically independent of the way that we conceive of those objects, then we can be quite short with these questions for objects that exist in reality. But, even if we make this supposition, we are still left to face the above questions in the case of objects that exist only in the understanding. And if we suppose that the properties that objects possess in the understanding do generally depend upon how those objects are conceived, then we are left to face the above questions for all objects. Since a case-by-case analysis is out of the question here, we shall move on to a largely impressionistic discussion of the premises of Anselm's argument.

Is it true that, if *that than which no greater can be conceived* exists in the understanding, then *that than which no greater can be conceived* can be conceived to exist in reality? This claim might not be true if objects in the understanding are *identified* by the properties that they possess, and if the properties of objects in the understanding are *determined* by the way in which those objects are conceived. Moreover, this claim might not be true if existence in the understanding requires coherent conception, and if *that than which no greater can be conceived* can only be coherently conceived to exist in the understanding alone.

Is it true that, if *that than which no greater can be conceived* exists in reality then *it* is greater than *it* would be if *it* were to exist only in the understanding? This claim can only be true if we can make sense of counterfactual claims about what objects that exist in reality would be like if they existed only in the understanding. But it is not entirely clear that we can make sense of such claims if we suppose that objects that exist both in the understanding and in reality have *the very same* properties in the understanding that they have in reality. Moreover, it is not obvious – at least, not to all – that existence in reality is properly thought of as a great-making property. At least some people find it plausible to suppose that the greatness of *that than which no greater can be conceived* does not depend upon whether it exists in reality (though it might depend upon whether it is *conceived* to exist in reality).

Does the interim conclusion at 3 follow from Premises 1 and 2? That's hard to say. If *that than which no greater can be conceived* exists only in the understanding, then it is certainly the case that *that than which no greater can be conceived* exists in the understanding. Given Premise 1, we can certainly conclude that, if *that than which no greater can be conceived* exists only in the understanding, then *that than which no greater can be conceived* can be conceived to exist in reality. Premise 2 tells us that, if *that than which no greater can be conceived* exists in reality then *it* is greater than *it* would be if *it* were to exist only in the understanding. Does it now follow that if *that than which no greater can be conceived* exists only in the understanding, then it is something than which a greater can be conceived?

Not obviously. Suppose, for example, that we think that the properties that an object has in the understanding depend upon how that object is conceived, and that the properties that an object has in the understanding can differ from the properties than that object has in reality (in those cases in which an object exists both in the understanding and in reality). Suppose, further, that we suppose that *existence in the understanding* and *existence in reality* are properties. Then, we might consistently suppose – for all that has been said to this point – that *that than which no greater can be conceived* exists only in the understanding; that in the understanding *that than which no greater can be conceived* possesses the property of existing in reality (though, of course, since it does not exist in reality, it does not possess that property in reality); that if that than which no greater can be conceived existed in reality it would be greater than it actually is (given that it exists only in the understanding); and that *that than which no greater can be conceived* is the greatest being in the understanding (and hence is such that no greater being than it can be conceived).

It may be that, if we make *other* theoretical choices, it will turn out that 3 does follow from 1 and 2 However, in order to determine whether that is so, there is no alternative but to work through the case-by-case analysis that we are here eschewing. Moreover, it is worth noting that, even if there are cases on which 3 follows from 1 and 2, there might be good reason not to accept the theses that characterize those cases. If the fool can reasonably opt for the kind of case that underlies the analysis in the previous paragraph, then it seems that the fool can reasonably claim that Anselm's argument is simply invalid.

Is it true that *that than which no greater can be conceived* is not something than which a greater can be conceived? Not obviously. If we suppose that the properties that an object has in the understanding do not depend upon how that object is conceived, and if we suppose that existence in reality is a sufficiently weighty great-making property, then we might suppose that, if *that than which no greater can be conceived* does not exist, then, merely by conceiving of a suitable thing that exists in reality, we conceive of a thing that is greater than *that than which no greater can be conceived*.

The upshot of the discussion of Anselm's argument to this point is, I think, that it is not easy to tell whether there is a set of theoretical assumptions – about the understanding, existence in the understanding, property possession in the understanding, the relationship between conceiving objects to possess certain properties and possession of properties by those objects in the understanding, the relationship between believing that objects possess certain properties and conceiving that those objects possess those properties, and so forth – relative to which the conclusion of Anselm's argument follows from the premises of that argument, and relative to which all of the premises of Anselm's argument are true. If it turns out that there is no such set of theoretical assumptions, then it seems that the right thing to say is that Anselm's argument is plainly unacceptable, but that it gains superficial plausibility because of slippage in the interpretation of key terms and slippage in the underlying theoretical assumptions that might be invoked in connection with each of the premises of the argument. On the other hand, if it turns out that there is such a set of theoretical assumptions, then, in order to determine whether the argument is then acceptable, we should at least need to determine whether the set of theoretical assumptions is itself acceptable. If, for example, the fool can reasonably reject *any* set of theoretical assumptions that would render Anselm's argument otherwise acceptable, then it seems that it would still be the case that the argument is ultimately unsuccessful: the argument would still fail to show that the fool is irrational in failing to accept the existence (in reality) of *that than which no greater can be conceived.*

Even if someone is prepared to accept the way that the discussion has gone to this point, such a person might still think that there are other ways in which it can be shown that Anselm's argument is plainly unacceptable. In particular, following the lead of Anselm's earliest critic, the Marmoutier monk Gaunilo, who wrote an almost immediate response *In Behalf of the Fool*, one might think that it can be shown on entirely independent grounds that Anselm's argument, if successful, would simply prove far too much. For suppose that someone offered the following argument:

> Even the fool is convinced that that island than which no greater island can be conceived is in the understanding, since when he hears this, he understands it; and whatever is understood is in the understanding. And certainly that island than which no greater island can be conceived cannot be in the understanding alone. For if it is even in the understanding alone, it can be conceived to exist in reality also, which is greater. Thus if that island than which no greater island can be conceived is in the understanding, then that island than which no greater island can be conceived is itself an island than which a greater island can be conceived. But surely this cannot be. Thus without doubt that island than which a greater island cannot be conceived exists, both in the understanding and in reality.

Surely we are entitled to think that there must be something wrong with this argument – surely we know that there is, in reality, no island than which no greater island can be conceived. Moreover, even if you happen to think that there is, in reality, an island than which no greater island can be conceived, surely you will concede that there are other kinds for which the corresponding claim is not plausible. There is, after all, nothing special about *islands*. If you think it false that there is a member of the Richmond Football Club than which no greater member of the Richmond Football Club can be conceived, then you can consider the variant of Anselm's argument that uses that example instead. (If we pair the latter example with another variant of Anselm's argument for the claim that there is a member of the Carlton Football Club than which no greater member of the Carlton Football Club can be conceived, then you might suspect that we get not merely absurdity but outright contradiction: for what would happen when these two were pitted against one another? A member of the Richmond Football Club than which no greater member of the Richmond Football Club can be conceived would certainly always outplay any member of the Carlton Football Club; and a member of the Carlton Football Club than which no greater member of the Carlton Football Club can be conceived would always outplay any member of the Richmond Football Club!)

In the face of this objection, the proponent of Anselm's argument needs to be able to point to a relevant difference between *that than which no greater can be conceived* and *that F than which no greater F can be conceived* (where 'F' is something other than 'being') that brings it about that, while Anselm's argument goes through, the parallel argument about *that F than which no greater F can be conceived* breaks down. There are not many options.

First, the proponent of Anselm's argument might try saying that, while the expression 'that than which no greater can be conceived' is understood, the expression 'that island than which no greater island can be conceived' is not understood. It is hard to see how this position could be defended. What possible reason could the fool have for allowing that only the former expression is understood?

Second, the proponent of Anselm's argument might try saying that, even if *that island than which no greater island can be conceived* exists in the understanding, it cannot be conceived to exist in reality (although *that than which no greater can be conceived* can be conceived to exist in reality). Again, it is hard to see how this position could be defended. What possible reason could the fool have for allowing this differential treatment of the two putative denizens of the understanding?

Third, the proponent of Anselm's argument might try saying that, while it is true that, if *that than which no greater can be conceived* exists in reality *it* is greater than *it* would be if *it* were to exist only in the understanding, it is not true that, if *that island than which no greater island can be conceived* exists in reality then *it* is greater than *it* would be if *it* were to exist only in the understanding. But, yet again, it is hard to see how this position could be defended. What possible reason could the fool have – and, more generally, what possible reason could there be – for allowing this differential treatment of the two prospective denizens of reality?

Finally, the proponent of Anselm's argument might try saying that, while *that than which no greater can be conceived* is not something than which a greater can be conceived, *that island than which no greater island can be conceived* is an island than which a greater island can be conceived. But, one final time, it is hard to see how this position could be defended. What possible reason could the fool have – and more generally, what possible reason could there be – for *this* differential treatment of *that than which no greater can be conceived*, and *that island than which no greater island can be conceived*?

Even if it is true that Gaunilo's objection defeats the argument that Anselm actually gave, it should not be thought that this must be the end of the line for Anselm's argument. The discussion to this point has taken the formulation of Anselm's argument entirely at face value: we've stuck to Anselm's actual text – under the particular translation that we've adopted for discussion – and to a straightforwardly literal interpretation of that text. But that leaves at least three kinds of options open.

First, it might be that there are other translations of Anselm's text that would yield better arguments. Second, it might be that there are less literal – more liberal – interpretations of Anselm's text that would yield better arguments. (Perhaps we should note here that there might be other ways of understanding the theoretical framework in which Anselm's argument was meant to be located that also contribute to the production of a better argument.) And, third, it might be that there other arguments that are more or less loosely inspired by – or, at any rate, partial causal products of – Anselm's text, but which yield a more satisfactory argument than the one that we have been considering.

In the time since Anselm produced his original argument, there has been discussion of many different arguments that fit into the three categories introduced in the preceding paragraph. There are many different 'interpretations' of Anselm's text that have been provided in the succeeding centuries; and there are many different 'ontological arguments' that are more or less loosely inspired by – or, at any rate, partial causal products of – Anselm's text.

Here, for example, are some recent 'formulations' of the argument from Proslogion *II*:

Adams (1971):

1. There is a thing x, and a magnitude m, such that x exists in the understanding, m is the magnitude of x, and it is not possible that there is

a thing y and a magnitude n such that n is the magnitude of y and n>m.

2. For any thing x and magnitude m, if x exists in the understanding, m is the magnitude of x, and it is not possible that there is a thing y and magnitude n such that n is the magnitude of y and n>m, then it is possible that x exists in reality.

3. For any thing x and magnitude m, if m is the magnitude of x, and it is not possible that there is a thing y and a magnitude n such that n is the magnitude of y and n>m, and x does not exist in reality, then it is not possible that if x exists in reality then there is a magnitude n such that n is greater than m and n is the magnitude of x.

4. (Hence) There is a thing x and a magnitude m such that x exists in the understanding, and x exists in reality, and m is the magnitude of x, and it is not possible that there is a thing y and a magnitude n such that n is the magnitude of y and n>m (From 1, 2 and 3).

Millican (2004):

1. The phrase 'a-nature-than-which-no-greater-nature-can-be-thought' is clearly understood by the Fool, and apparently makes sense.

2. If a phrase 'A' is clearly understood and apparently makes sense, then we can take it to successfully denote some specific nature.

3. A nature which is instantiated in reality is greater than one which is not instantiated in nature.

4. It is obviously impossible to think of a nature that is greater than a-nature-than-which-no-greater-nature-can-be-thought.

5. (Hence), a-nature-than-which-no-greater-nature-can-be-thought must indeed be instantiated in reality (From 1, 2, 3 and 4).

Leftow (2005):

1. Someone thinks of a possible object which is something than which no greater can be thought.

2. If a possible something than which no greater can be thought is thought of but not actual, it could have been greater than it actually is.

3. (So) There actually exists something than which no greater can be thought (From 1 and 2).

And here are some examples of 'ontological arguments' that are more or less loosely inspired by – or, at any rate, partial causal products of – Anselm's text:

Curley (1978, expounding Descartes):

1. I have ideas of things that, whether or not they exist, and whether or not I think of them, have true and immutable natures or essences (Premise).
2. Whatever property I perceive clearly and distinctly as belonging to the true and immutable nature of something I have an idea of really does belong to that thing (Premise).
3. I have an idea of God as a supremely perfect being (Premise).
4. I perceive clearly and distinctly that existence belongs to the true and immutable nature of a supremely perfect being (Premise).
5. (Hence) A supremely perfect being really does exist (From 1–4).

Plantinga (1974):

1. For any x, x is *maximally excellent* iff x is omnipotent, omniscient and perfectly good (Definition).
2. For any x, x is *maximally great* iff x is necessarily existent and maximally excellent (Definition).
3. It is possible that there is a maximally great entity (Premise).
4. (Hence) There is a maximally excellent entity (From 3).

Anderson (1990, expounding Gödel):

1. For any x, x is *God-like* iff x has as essential properties those and only those properties that are positive (Definition).
2. For any x, and any A, A is an *essence* of x iff, for every property B, x has B necessarily iff A entails B (Definition).
3. For any x, x *necessarily exists* iff every essence of x is necessarily exemplified (Definition).
4. For any property P, if P is positive, then the negation of P is not positive (Premise).
5. Any property entailed by a positive property is positive (Premise).

6. The property of being God-like is positive (Premise).
7. For any property P, if P is positive, then P is necessarily positive (Premise).
8. Necessary existence is positive (Premise).
9. (Hence) Necessarily, the property of being God-like is exemplified (From 4–8).

In my opinion, the only proper response to these arguments is to treat each of them in the way that I treated the argument that I derived from Anselm's text. That is, the only proper response to each of these arguments is to ask, of each of them, (a) whether it is true that the conclusion of the argument is a (logical) consequence of its premises; (b) whether it is true that the premises of the argument have the kind of standing that would make it appropriate to say that the argument really is a proof of its conclusion; and (c) whether it is right to think that the conclusion of the argument suffices to establish the existence of God. Only a careful investigation of these kinds of questions can issue in a fair assessment of these arguments (and, of course, that is not something that we can hope to do in the course of the present investigation, even for the small sample of 'ontological arguments' given above).

Because the proper assessment of arguments is sensitive to the slightest changes in formulations, there are no easy generalizations that can be made about 'ontological arguments'. Some 'ontological arguments' fail because their conclusions are only mistakenly supposed by their proponents to be logical consequences of their premises. Some 'ontological arguments' fail because their premises are only mistakenly supposed by their proponents to have the kind of standing that would make it appropriate to say that they belong to successful arguments. Some ontological arguments fail because they only suffice to establish the existence of some uncontroversial entity that is plainly to be distinguished from God. Moreover, each of these kinds of failings can take a number of different forms: some 'ontological arguments' trade on equivocation; some 'ontological arguments' simply involve mistakes in inference; some 'ontological arguments' have premises that it is obvious that those who do not believe in God reasonably reject; some 'ontological arguments' fail because they have premises that it could only be reasonable to accept if it were reasonable to believe in God; some 'ontological arguments' fail because their conclusion establishes no more than that the physical universe exists; and so forth.

While there is a fairly broad consensus that no 'ontological argument' that has appeared thus far is a successful argument, and while there is almost universal agreement that no 'ontological argument' that has appeared thus far is such that no-one could reject its conclusion on pain of conviction of irrationality, there is considerable disagreement about the future prospects for 'ontological arguments'. Some philosophers think that there is reason to be optimistic or, at any rate, not very pessimistic, about the prospects of discovery of a successful 'ontological argument'. Other philosophers hold that, while it can hardly be ruled out *a priori* that there is a successful 'ontological argument', there is good reason – based both in the failings detected in 'ontological arguments' that have been hitherto been produced and in independent reasons for thinking that God does not exist – to think that it is highly unlikely that there are any such arguments. Yet other philosophers think that there are good *a priori* reasons for supposing that there simply cannot be successful 'ontological arguments'.

There are two kinds of strategies that might be pursued by those who think that there are good *a priori* reasons for supposing that there simply cannot be successful 'ontological arguments'. On the one hand, such philosophers might try to argue that it is clear that every possible 'ontological argument' is vulnerable to a Gaunilo-style critique. On the other hand, such philosophers might try to argue that every possible 'ontological argument' must try to do something that is *a priori* impossible – for example, build an *a priori* bridge between the realm of concepts and the realm of actually existing objects – or appeal to a principle that is *a priori* indefensible – for example, the claim that existence is a real or genuine property of things.

Notoriously, Immanuel Kant declared that we can know *a priori* that ontological proof of the existence of God is impossible. Many people, in the centuries that have passed since Kant wrote on this topic, have been happy to declare that Kant showed that 'ontological arguments' fail – or that 'the ontological argument' fails – because 'existence is not a real predicate'. However, when we look closely at what Kant has to say in the Second Division, Book II, Chapter III, Section IV of *The Critique of Pure Reason*, it is very hard to see how to so much as *apply* what he says there to most of the examples in the selection of 'ontological arguments' set out above.

Kant's critique of 'the famous ontological argument of Descartes' draws on his own controversial views about concepts, judgments, predicates, possibilities, his analytic/synthetic distinction, objects, experience, existence and so forth. Moreover, Kant's critique is not developed in connection with a specific formulation of 'the famous ontological argument of Descartes': in *The Critique of Pure Reason*, Kant does not exhibit a particular formulation of the Cartesian argument and then say where exactly it is that the particular formulation falls down. Rather, what Kant does is to argue – in various different ways – that there is no way in which one can move *a priori* from the concept of an object to the justified belief that there is an object that falls under the concept. Hence, in particular, according to Kant, there is no way in which one can move *a priori* from the concept of a supremely perfect being – or the concept of *that than which no greater can be conceived* – to the justified belief that a supremely perfect being, or *that than which no greater can be conceived*, exists.

Should we suppose that the 'ontological arguments' set out above involve *a priori* movement from concept to belief? Consider, for example, Plantinga's argument. Setting aside the two definitions that give content to the notion of a maximally great entity, the argument consists of a single inference from a single premise to a conclusion. It is, we may suppose, knowable *a priori* that the inference is valid. The premise might be held to be knowable *a priori*; but, depending upon the purposes of the defender of the arguer, it might also be held to be knowable only *a posteriori*. Plantinga himself thinks that the argument can, at best, establish only that it can be reasonable for people to accept the conclusion of the argument, and, for that purpose, it seems clear that there is no reason to suppose that the premise is knowable *a priori*. But, if that's right, then it seems that Plantinga's argument doesn't involve *a priori* movement from concept to belief, and so, at the very least, it is not obvious that Plantinga's argument is even *prima facie* vulnerable to Kant's criticisms.

Perhaps it might be objected that it is unfair to require that Kant's criticisms should defeat Plantinga's argument, at least given the purpose that Plantinga has for his argument. But we can ask the same questions about, say, Curley's exposition of Descartes' *Meditation V* argument. Is it true that this argument involves *a priori* movement from concept to belief?

It seems clear that Kant would be happy enough to concede the first and third premises to Descartes: Kant accepts that we do have an idea of God as a supremely perfect being, and, though this is perhaps more debatable, that we do have ideas of things that, whether or not they exist, and whether or not we think of them, have true and immutable natures or essences. Moreover, it seems that Kant can hardly deny that the conclusion follows from the premises: the conclusion of the argument certainly seems to be a logical consequence of the premises. Is it plausible to suggest that a proper target for Kant's criticism may be found in either the second or the fourth premise? Kant himself seems to indicate that he is happy with the second premise: he allows that we know *a priori* that God is omnipotent. Generalizing from this case, it seems that he will be happy to allow that whatever property is perceived clearly and distinctly as belonging to the true and immutable nature of something that we have an idea of really does belong to that thing. So it seems that Kant must object to the fourth premise, that is, to the claim that we perceive clearly and distinctly that existence belongs to the true and immutable nature of a supremely perfect being.

Does justified acceptance of the premise that we perceive clearly and distinctly that existence belongs to the true and immutable nature of a supremely perfect being require *a priori* movement from concept to belief? Does justified acceptance of the premise that we perceive clearly and distinctly that existence belongs to the true and immutable nature of a supremely perfect being require acceptance of the claim that existence is a real predicate (i.e. acceptance of the claim that existence can be part of the concept of a thing)? I think that it is not straightforward to answer these questions. Moreover, even if we do think that this formulation of Descartes' argument is at least *prima facie* vulnerable to Kant's criticisms, it still remains to be determined whether Kant's criticisms constitute a weighty objection to the argument in question. Should we think, for example, that the only way in which it could be true that we perceive clearly and distinctly that existence belongs to the true and immutable nature of a supremely perfect being is if it were true that the concept of a supremely perfect being somehow contains existence? If we suppose, as perhaps Descartes himself would have allowed, that we can clearly and distinctly perceive that a property belongs to the true and immutable nature of a thing even though the property in question is no part of our concept of that thing, then it seems that we shall still be able to conclude that, in the end, Curley's formulation of Descartes' ontological argument is not damaged by the Kantian criticism.

Even if we are persuaded that Kant failed to show that ontological proof of the existence of God is impossible, it remains possible, for all that has been argued to this point, that there is some other way of showing that ontological proof of the existence of God is impossible. In particular, as we noted earlier, it might be that it is possible to mount a strong case for the claim that every possible ontological argument is vulnerable to Gaunilo-style critique.

Consider, for example, Plantinga's argument. Suppose that we identify some properties that make for excellence in islands – the I-properties. Suppose, further, that the I-max properties are the ideal, or maximal – versions of the I-properties. Then we can mount the following argument:

1. For any x, x is *maximally I-excellent* iff x possesses the I-max properties (Definition).
2. For any x, x is *maximally I-great* iff x is necessarily existent and maximally I-excellent (Definition).
3. It is possible that there is a maximally I-great entity (Premise).
4. (Hence) There is a maximally I-excellent entity (From 3).

This argument seems as well-suited to the purposes of the opponent of Plantinga's ontological argument as Gaunilo's argument is to the purposes of the opponent of Anselm's argument. Moreover, one might suspect that it won't require much ingenuity to carry out the same trick for other ontological arguments. However, it is no easy matter to show that there *could not* be an ontological argument that is not vulnerable to this kind of objection. As things now stand, it is at least a highly controversial question whether Gödel's ontological argument is vulnerable to this kind of objection, and it seems that it must be an open question whether there are kinds of ontological arguments that we have not yet countenanced that are immune to Gaunilo-style critique.

In view of the preceding considerations, I am inclined to think that we do not now, and perhaps never will, have good *a priori* reasons for rejecting the claim that there are successful ontological arguments. However, for reasons that I have argued at length elsewhere, I also think that it is quite clear that no ontological argument that has hitherto been produced comes anywhere near success. In my view, when we look in detail at the premises and conclusions of those ontological arguments that have been produced to date, we do find either (a) that the conclusions are not adequately supported by the premises; or (b) the premises don't have the kind of status that is possessed by premises is successful arguments; or (c) the conclusion of the argument is something that non-believers can accept with equanimity. But, of course, in order to decide whether I am right about this, there is no substitute for a detailed examination of all of the arguments in question.

Bibliography

Adams, R. (1971) 'The Logical Structure of Anselm's Argument' *Philosophical Review* 80, 28–54.

Anderson, C. (1990) 'Some Emendations on Gödel's Ontological Proof' *Faith and Philosophy* 7, 291–303.

Barnes, J. (1972) *The Ontological Argument* London: Macmillan.

Charlesworth, M. (1965) *St. Anselm's Proslogion* Oxford: Oxford University Press.

Curley, E. (1978) *Descartes against the Sceptics* Oxford: Blackwell, 125–69.

Descartes, R. (1968/1637) *Discourse on Method and the Meditations*, trans. with an introduction by F. Sutcliffe, Harmondsworth: Penguin.

Dombrowski, D. (2006) *Rethinking the Ontological Argument: A Neoclassical Response* Cambridge: Cambridge University Press.

Harrelson, K. (2009) *The Ontological Argument from Descartes to Hegel* Amherst: Prometheus Books.

Hartshorne, C. (1965) *Anselm's Discovery: A Re-Examination of the Ontological Proof of God's Existence* La Salle, Ill.: Open Court.

Leftow, B. (2005) 'The Ontological Argument' in W. Wainwright (ed.) *The Oxford Handbook of Philosophy of Religion* Oxford: Oxford University Press, 80–115.

Lewis, D. (1970) 'Anselm and Actuality' *Noûs* 4, 175–88.

Mann, W. (1972) 'The Ontological Presuppositions of the Ontological Argument' *Review of Metaphysics* 26, 260–77.

Millican, P. (2004) 'The One Fatal Flaw in Anselm's Argument' *Mind* 113, 451, 437–476.

Oppy, G. (1995) *Ontological Arguments and Belief in God* Cambridge: Cambridge University Press.

Oppy, G. (2006) *Arguing about Gods* Cambridge: Cambridge University Press.

Plantinga, A. (1974) *The Nature of Necessity* Oxford: Oxford University Press.

Sobel, J. (2004) *Logic and Theism: Arguments for and against Beliefs in God* Cambridge: Cambridge University Press.

CHAPTER 4

AQUINAS AND THE COSMOLOGICAL ARGUMENT
William L. Rowe

The first three of Aquinas's 'Five Ways' constitute three distinct, important versions of the Cosmological Argument.[1] If we use the translation of the Blackfriars edition, the first way proceeds as follows:

> The first and most obvious way is based on change. Some things in the world are certainly in process of change: this we plainly see. Now anything in process of change is being changed by something else. This is so because it is characteristic of things in process of change that they do not yet have the perfection towards which they move, though able to have it; whereas it is characteristic of something causing change to have that perfection already. For to cause change is to bring into being what was previously only able to be, and this can only be done by something that already is: thus fire, which is actually hot, causes wood, which is able to be hot, to become actually hot, and in this way causes change in the wood. Now the same thing cannot at the same time be both actually X and potentially X, though it can be actually X and potentially Y: the actually hot cannot at the same time be potentially hot, though it can be potentially cold. Consequently, a thing in process of change cannot itself cause that same change; it cannot change itself. Of necessity therefore anything in process of change is being changed by something else.
>
> Moreover, this something else, if in process of change, is itself being changed by yet another thing; and this last by another. Now we must stop somewhere, otherwise there will be no first cause of the change, and, as a result, no subsequent causes. For it is only when acted upon by the first cause that the intermediate causes will produce the change: if the hand does not move the stick, the stick will not move anything else. Hence one is bound to arrive at some first cause of change not itself being changed by anything, and this is what everybody understands by God.[2]

Before examining the structure of this argument, we need to note that this is only the first part of the Cosmological Argument: that is, an argument to establish the existence of an unchanged changer, a first cause of change, which itself is not in a process of change. After concluding his argument for the unchanged changer, Aquinas simply adds 'and this is what everybody understands by God'. But, of course, there is a serious question as to whether an unchanged changer need have the properties of the theistic God. It would be unfair to Aquinas, however, to charge him with simply assuming that an unchanged changer would have to be God. For in other sections of the *Summa Theologica,* Aquinas presents rational arguments designed to demonstrate that the unchanged changer must possess the properties associated with the theistic concept of God.[3] The argument to establish the existence of an unchanged changer represents, therefore, a major version of the *first part* of the Cosmological Argument. The complete development of the Cosmological Argument in Aquinas's *Summa Theologica* extends far beyond his brief statement of the first three ways.

By 'change' Aquinas means to include change in place, change in quantity (e.g. something becoming larger or smaller), and change in quality (e.g. something changing from being cold to being hot). The argument, I believe, is more forceful when the change in question is of the third sort, change in quality; but in appraising the argument I shall not limit the discussion to examples of qualitative change. The argument begins with a fact about the world that experience teaches us: some things change.

1. *Some things are in a process of change.*

The next premise in the argument represents what Aquinas would view as a metaphysical principle established by *a priori* reasoning, rather than a fact established by experience.

2. *Whatever is in a process of change is being changed by something else.*

Aquinas recognizes the need to establish this premise and, there-fore, tries to support it by an argument. We shall examine his argument for (2) below.

3. *An infinite regress of changers, each changed by another is impossible.*

(3) has often been denied by critics of the argument. We shall examine (3) and Aquinas's argument for it.

Therefore:

4. *There is a first cause of change, itself not in a process of change.*

The core of this argument, as Aquinas clearly recognized, consists of the two claims: that whatever is changing is being changed by something else, and that an infinite regress of changers, each changed by another, is impossible. Let us begin our analysis of the argument by examining Aquinas's argument in support of premise (2).

If something is in a process of qualitative change then, on Aquinas's view, it is coming to be in a certain state that it is not now actually in. For example, if the water in the kettle is changing from being cold to being boiling hot, then it can be said to be coming to be in the state of being boiling hot, but just so long as it is *coming to be* in that state, it is not yet in that state, but in a state somewhere between cold and boiling hot. Now if something is not actually in a certain state but can come to be in that state – as water that is not actually hot nevertheless can become hot – it is, in Aquinas's view, *potentially* in that state, but not *actually* in it. Thus cold water is potentially hot but not actually hot, and hot water is potentially cold, but not actually cold. These considerations lead Aquinas to the principle that nothing can be both actually and potentially in the same state at the same time. 'Now the same thing cannot at the same time be both actually X and potentially X, though it can be actually X and potentially Y: the actually hot cannot at the same time be potentially hot, though it can be potentially cold'. So far Aquinas's reasoning seems cogent, but we are still a major step away from establishing that whatever is in a process of change is being changed, by something else.

We come now to the crucial step in Aquinas's argument for premise (2). Aquinas claims that if something is *in* a process of change towards a state A, there must be something *actually in state A* that is causing the thing in question to be changing towards state A. This is the most plausible interpretation of his remark: 'For to cause change is to bring into being what was previously only able to be, and this can only be done by something that already is: thus fire, which is actually hot, causes wood, which is able to be hot, to become actually hot, and in this way causes change in the wood'.

There are two major objections to this fundamental claim in Aquinas's reasoning in support of premise (2). But before considering these objections, we need to see the basic role Aquinas's claim plays in his argument for premise (2). That argument may be exhibited as follows:

i. *If something is in a process of change towards a state A, then it is potentially in state A.*
ii. *If something is in a process of change towards state A, there must be something which is actually in state A which is causing the thing in question to be changing towards state A.*
iii. *Nothing can be both actually in state A and potentially in state A at the same time.*

Therefore:

2. Whatever is in a process of change is being changed by something else.

As I noted above, there are two major objections to the crucial step (ii) in Aquinas's argument for (2). First, it does not seem to be universally true that if one thing causes a second thing to change towards a certain state, the first thing must actually be in that state. It does seem true that if something makes water become hot, it must itself be hot. But suppose a plant is in a process of dying. Must that which causes the plant to be changing towards the state of being dead be something that itself is already actually dead? Moreover, doesn't Aquinas believe that God can directly cause cold water to become hot? But it makes no sense to say that God is in the state of being hot. Perhaps Aquinas only meant to assert that if one thing causes a second thing to be changing towards a certain state, the first thing must actually be in that state or have all that state represents in another form. Thus, although God is not actually hot, He has all the power that is represented by the state of heat. However, once we begin to qualify Aquinas's basic principle in this way, the principle becomes vague to a degree that renders it difficult to understand exactly what is being asserted and it becomes less clear that a thing cannot cause a change to take place in itself. Thus, according to the first objection, if we take Aquinas's principle literally there seem to be counter-examples to it. On the other hand, if we try to qualify the principle by not insisting that the cause *actually* be in the state it is causing another to change towards, the principle becomes vague and difficult to understand with the result that it becomes less than certain that a thing cannot cause itself to change towards a certain state. For while it is clear that nothing can be both actually and potentially in a given state at the same time, it is not so clear that a thing might have the power or degree of reality represented by a certain state even though it is not actually in that state.

It is not difficult to see the fundamental idea underlying Aquinas's reasoning. If something undergoes a change and, as a result, comes to have some feature it did not previously possess, it would seem that the only way it could get this feature is from something that already has it. Since it itself did not have it, it cannot have been the cause of the change it underwent in coming to acquire it. Nor could anything else that lacked that feature have caused this thing to come to acquire that feature. To suppose otherwise would be to suppose that something comes from nothing. Consequently, whatever causes a thing to come to possess something must be a thing that already has that something and, hence, can impart it to the thing that is undergoing a change.

As attractive as this fundamental idea seems to be, it conceals an assumption of enormous importance, and it is the point of the second major objection to bring this assumption to the surface. We can get at this assumption best by noting that Aquinas considers only two alternatives in discussing the fact that some things are in a process of change. He considers the possibility that a thing might be the cause of its own process of change, and he considers the possibility that something else might be the cause of the change that a thing is undergoing. What he does not consider is a third possibility: namely, that it is simply a brute fact that certain things are changing. Of course, we know that many things which are changing are being changed by other things – thus the water is being changed from cold to hot by something else, the fire. But the question is: Why may not there be some things in a process of change that are neither causing themselves to change nor being changed by other things? Suppose we say that it is a *brute fact* that X is changing just in case X is changing but there is no thing that is causing it to change. And the question is: What reasons does Aquinas give for ruling out the possibility that it is a brute fact that certain things are changing? The answer is that Aquinas gives no reasons for ruling out this possibility. He simply does not consider it a genuine possibility. Thus after ruling out the possibility that a thing causes itself to change, Aquinas immediately infers: 'Of necessity therefore anything in process of change is being changed by something else'. Underlying this inference is a basic assumption, namely, *that it is never a brute fact that something is changing.*

The second major objection calls this assumption into question. Why should we believe that it is never a brute fact that something is changing? Of course, if there were such a brute fact, then there would be some fact that is without any causal explanation. And if a causal explanation is the only form of explanation appropriate when the fact in question is some thing changing from one state to another, then to admit brute facts is to admit facts that are unintelligible in the sense that they admit of no explanation. But again: Why not admit that some facts involving change are ultimate in the sense that while they may enter into an explanation of other facts, they themselves have no explanation whatever? Having raised this question in the form of an objection to Aquinas's reasoning for premise (2), we need pursue it no further for the moment. For the moment it is sufficient to note that Aquinas is assuming for purposes of his argument that there are no brute facts involving qualitative change. The point of the objection is simply to bring this assumption to the surface and to question its truth.

Thus far Aquinas has argued that some things are in a process of change and whatever is in a process of change is being changed by something else. Now if we start with something that is in a process of change, we must, in tracing the causes of its process of change, be faced either with an infinite regress of changers, each in a process of change and therefore being changed by something else, or the regress must terminate somewhere in a cause of change that itself is unchanging. The final step in Aquinas's argument is to establish that:

3. *An infinite regress of changers, each changed by another is impossible.*

His argument is that if there is no first cause of change, itself unchanging, there cannot be anything in a process of change. 'For it is only when acted upon by the first cause that the intermediate causes will produce the change: if the hand does not move the stick, the stick will not move anything else'. On the surface, it must be admitted that Aquinas's argument appears to be nothing more than a rather crude instance of question-begging. We want to know why Aquinas thinks the series must terminate in a first changer, itself unchanging, rather than regressing to infinity, each cause of change itself in a process of change and, therefore, being changed by something else. In response to our inquiry, Aquinas in effect says nothing more than that, in a series *which has a first member*, if that first member does not cause change then there will be no process of change in any member of the series. And this seems true enough. But, of course, our question was not why *in a series with a first member* the first member must be causing change in order for other members in the series to be in a process of change, but why need there be a first member in a series in which there are members in a process of change. In giving the answer he does, Aquinas appears to *assume* that every series in which there are members in a process of change *has a first member*. But this is precisely the issue he has undertaken to establish. Hence, his argument begs the very question at issue.

When a philosopher of the stature of Aquinas offers an argument that appears to be a textbook example of a question-begging argument, it is sometimes wise to search for something beneath the surface that may have been poorly expressed but, nevertheless, may represent his real view on the subject. Although, as stated, Aquinas's argument is, I believe, question-begging, perhaps there is more to his view than meets the eye. In any case, at the risk of misinterpreting Aquinas, I shall suggest a line of reasoning against the infinite regress that may represent at least part of his view on the subject. However, since Aquinas again argues against the infinite regress in the second way and since the interpretation I wish to suggest is more easily presented in connection with the second way, I shall postpone its development for the moment.

In the second way, Aquinas again argues from causation. But here it is the cause of a thing's existence and not of a process of change taking place within an existing thing that is the initial focus of his attention.

The second way is based on the nature of causation. In the observable world causes are found to be ordered in series; we never observe, nor ever could, something causing itself, for this would mean it preceded itself, and this is not possible. Such a series of causes must however stop somewhere; for in it an earlier member causes an intermediate and the intermediate a last (whether the intermediate be one or many). Now if you eliminate a cause you also eliminate its effects, so that you cannot have a last cause, nor an intermediate one, unless you have a first. Given therefore no stop in the series of causes, and hence no first cause, there would be no intermediate causes either, and no last effect, and this would be an open mistake. One is therefore forced to suppose some first cause, to which everyone gives the name 'God'.[4]

Perhaps the first point that comes to mind – or, more accurately, strikes the eye – when the second way is compared with the first is that the second way is a much shorter argument. The reason for this is clear. In each way there are two points to be established. First, that nothing can be its own cause; second, that an infinite regress of causes is impossible. Now in the second way, the first point is obvious. For in the second way, it is the existence of a thing we are initially inquiring about, and it seems obvious that nothing can be the cause of its own existence. Thus in the second way the first point to be established is so obvious as not to require much in the way of argument. In the first way, however, it is not a thing's existence that is the initial object of inquiry, but the fact that an existing thing is in a process of change towards some state, and it is far from obvious that something cannot cause itself to undergo a change. Hence, Aquinas feels compelled to present a fairly elaborate argument to establish the first way, and this accounts for the fact that the first way is double the length of the second.

Aquinas's second way may be stated as follows:

1. Some things exist and their existence is caused.
2. Whatever is caused to exist is caused to exist by something else.
3. An infinite regress of causes resulting in the existence of a particular thing is impossible.

Therefore:

4. There is a first cause of existence.

It is apparent that the second way has a similar structure to the first way. Each argument has three premises, the first of which asserts a fairly simple fact that is verified by our experience of the world. Then come two premises, one asserting that nothing causes itself to change (first way) or to exist (second way); and the other denying the possibility of an infinite regress of causes of change (first way) or of existence (second way). Finally, we have the conclusion asserting that there exists an unchanging cause of change (first way) or an uncaused cause of existence (second way).

Before we take up Aquinas's rejection of the infinite regress of causes of existence, one important difference between the first and second way should be noted. We pointed out a fundamental assumption underlying Aquinas's reasoning in the first way: that whenever a process of change occurs in a thing, something must cause that process of change. There can be no brute facts involving a process of change. The analogue to this assumption in the second way is that if something exists, something must cause that thing to exist. But no such assumption is required by Aquinas's reasoning in the second way. The reason for this is that the second premise of the second way is not 'Whatever exists is caused to exist by something else' but 'Whatever is caused to exist is caused to exist by something else'. In order to prove the latter, all Aquinas need rule out is that something should be the cause of its own existence – and this he does by simply noting that if a thing caused its own existence it would have to precede itself, which, of course, is impossible.

We come again to the central issue in the first two ways: Aquinas's argument against an infinite regress of causes. The argument for this conclusion in the second way appears to be nothing more than a repetition of the question-begging argument we encountered in the first way. I suggested earlier, however, that there may be something more substantial beneath the surface of his argument against an infinite regress of causes; it is now time to pursue this matter.

The surface impression one gets from Aquinas's argument against the infinite regress of causes is that he holds that, whenever we have a series of causes of changes in existing things (first way) or a series of causes resulting in the existence of something (second way), the series must have a *first member*. Thus, for example, if one human being is generated by other human beings, and they in turn by still others, the impression his argument conveys is that each such series of generators of existence must stop with a first member, it cannot regress to infinity.

But this is not Aquinas's view. Indeed, he explicitly rejects the view that the generation of one human by others could not proceed to infinity – 'it is not impossible for a man to be generated by man to infinity; . . .'[5] It is clear, then, that the impression given by Aquinas's argument against the infinite regress of causes does not represent his view. It must be that he thinks that only some regresses of causes cannot proceed to infinity. In order, then, to understand his argument, we need to distinguish those regresses of causes that he thinks may proceed to infinity from those he thinks cannot.

Unfortunately Aquinas says little to help us in this matter. He does say that in efficient causes it is impossible to proceed to infinity *per se*, but possible to proceed to infinity accidentally as regard efficient causes. Apparently, then, when we have a series of efficient causes, the series may be a *per se* series or an *accidental* series. If the former, it must have a first member; if the latter, it may proceed to infinity. The series of causes envisaged in the first and second ways must, therefore, be *per se* series of causes.

Notes

1 The first two ways, as we shall see, share a common style of reasoning.
2 *Summa Theologica*, 1a, 2, 3.
3 See Father Copleston's remark on this issue in *A History of Philosophy*, II (Westminister: The Newman Press, 1960), 342–343.
4 *Summa Theologica*, 1a, 2, 3.
5 *Summa Theologica*, 1a, 46, 2.

CHAPTER 5

WILLIAM PALEY AND THE ARGUMENT FROM DESIGN

Mark Wynn

Introduction

William Paley is sure to be mentioned in any introductory survey of the argument from design, and there is no doubting that he enjoys a secure place in the history of discussion of the argument. However, there is disagreement about the philosophical significance of his work. Robert Hurlbutt suggests that David Hume's *Dialogues Concerning Natural Religion*, published in 1779, constitute 'the *last* act in the drama of the design argument', and that what was to follow was merely 'a nineteenth-century curtain call in the work of Paley . . .'[1] On the other side, even as fierce a critic of the design argument as Richard Dawkins finds that Paley's arguments were unrefutable in his day. He comments that it was Darwin who 'made it possible to be an intellectually fulfilled atheist'[2] – and not, we may surmise, Hume.

These differing assessments suggest two kinds of question that we might put to Paley's work. First, to what extent are his reflections vulnerable to Hume's critique of natural theology? And second, supposing that his case has not been overturned pre-emptively by Hume, can Paley's version of the design argument be of more than antiquarian interest for a post-Darwinian readership? But before turning to these questions, let's put Paley in his historical context a little, and set out the main elements of his argument from design.

Historical context

William Paley was born in Peterborough, in England, in 1743, and he died in 1805. His father was a clergyman and teacher, and the younger Paley followed his father's example in both respects. He studied at the University of Cambridge, and in 1761 was awarded the Bunting Scholarship, the University's most prestigious mathematical prize.[3] His best-known work is the *Natural Theology or Evidences of the Existence and Attributes of the Deity Collected from the Appearances of Nature*, first published in 1802. It is here that he formulates in detail his version of the argument from design. The *Natural Theology* was to become a standard work on the curriculum at Cambridge, and Darwin read it when he enrolled at Christ's, as Paley had before him. Indeed, we might plausibly speculate that Darwin's own interest in the phenomena of biological adaptation was sparked, at least in part, by his reading of Paley. When recalling his days at Cambridge, he remarked of the *Natural Theology* and another of Paley's books that: 'The careful study of these works . . . was the only part of the Academical Course which . . . was of the least use to me in the education of my mind'![4]

The argument from design has, of course, a long and distinguished history. It can be traced back to the origins of Western philosophy in the thought of the pre-Socratics, and Plato defends a version of the argument in Book X of the *Laws*.[5] Paley's more immediate intellectual context was provided by figures such as William Derham, whose *Physico-Theology* was published in London in 1720, and John Ray, whose *The Wisdom of God Manifested in the Work of Creation* reached its 11th edition in 1743.[6] These writers were also interested in the idea of a providential order in nature and in the movements of the heavenly bodies. So when Paley takes up his pen, there is an already established tradition of English theology which draws its inspiration from observation of nature. And Paley's own work was to inspire further ventures of this kind, most famously in the Bridgewater Treatises of the 1830s.[7]

Of course, there is also a socio-economic as well as an intellectual context for Paley's writings. This is provided most obviously by the technological advances of the time. Human beings were constructing mechanisms of ever greater complexity, and at the same time they were coming to an ever greater appreciation of the intricate structure of the physical world, and especially of organisms; and it was natural to associate these two developments, and to see the world, as disclosed in scientific enquiry, as an intricately engineered structure. Famously, Paley made this connection by comparing the universe, or certain parts of it anyway, to a watch. This particular analogy was not novel to him;[8] indeed Hume draws the same comparison in the *Dialogues*.[9] However, despite his obvious dependence on this broader tradition of thought, the detailed texture of Paley's argument is manifestly his own. His case in the *Natural Theology* is developed at great length – the two volumes of the 2nd edition run to more than 500 pages – and Paley seems to be only occasionally dependent on the philosophical literature of the day. Moreover, as we shall see, his formulation of the watch example is careful, and not to be confused with any crude appeal to analogy.

The central argument

Let's turn now to an examination of the case that Paley assembles at such length in the *Natural Theology*. At the very beginning of this work, Paley sets down, famously, his version of the watch example. Much of the remainder of the book is spent documenting the structure of organisms, and the workings of the natural world in other respects. When he turns to these examples, Paley evidently wants his readers to refer back to his discussion of the watch, and to see that explanation in terms of design is appropriate in both cases, for much the same reasons. So Paley's formulation of the watch example is crucial for the later development of his argument, and it is worth quoting at some length, therefore:

> In crossing a heath, suppose I pitched my foot against a *stone*, and were asked how the stone came to be there; I might possibly answer, that, for any thing I knew to the contrary, it had lain there for ever: nor would it perhaps be very easy to show the absurdity of this answer. But suppose I had found a *watch* upon the ground, and it should be inquired how the watch happened to be in that place; I should hardly think of the answer which I had before given, that for any thing I knew, the watch might have always been there. Yet why should not this answer serve for the watch as well as for the stone? why is it not admissible in the second case, as in the first? For this reason, and no other, viz. that, when we come to

inspect the watch, we perceive (what we could not discover in the stone) that its several parts are framed and put together for a purpose, *e.g.* that they are so formed and adjusted as to produce motion, and that motion so regulated as to point out the hour of the day; that if the parts had been differently shaped from what they are, of a different size from what they are, or placed after any other manner, or in any other order, than that in which they are placed, either no motion at all would have been carried on in the machine, or none which would have answered the use that is now served by it . . . We take notice that the wheels are made of brass in order to keep them from rust: the springs of steel, no other metal being so elastic; that over the face of the watch there is placed a glass, a material employed in no other part of the work, but in the room of which, if there had been any other than a transparent substance, the hour could not be seen without opening the case. This mechanism being observed . . . the inference, we think, is inevitable, that the watch must have had a maker: that there must have existed, at some time, and at some place or other, an artificer or artificers, who formed it for the purpose which we find it actually to answer; who compre- hended its construction, and designed its use.[10]

It is clear that Paley intends the watch in this example to stand for anything whose parts interact with one another so as to serve a purpose. The fact that the parts of the watch serve a purpose allows us to see why they *can* be explained by reference to an 'artificer': in grasping the purpose, we see that a designer could have reason to assemble such a structure. But by itself, this consideration is not enough to show that the idea of design presents the *best* explanation of the watch's structure. To sustain this conclusion, we will need to think about the viability of other, rival explanations. It is this further question which Paley is aiming to address when he writes: 'if the parts had been differently shaped from what they are, of a different size from what they are . . . either no motion at all would have been carried on in the machine, or none which would have answered the use that is now served by it'. Here Paley is saying that there is a highly sensitive relationship between the organization of the parts of the watch and their capacity to serve this particular purpose. It is because he wants to establish this claim that Paley discusses at some length the various respects in which precisely this arrangement of parts is required to secure the effect of keeping and then telling the time. As he says, if the wheels of the watch had been made from some material other than brass, then the structure would not have served the purpose of time-keeping so well, because it would then have been liable to rust. And so on for the various other examples which he records (not all of which I have reproduced here). In each of these cases, Paley wants the reader to think, we can see how this arrangement of parts, or choice of materials, serves a goal; and we can see how the achievement of this goal is dependent upon precisely this disposition of the parts.

To use the language of more recent discussion, we might say that Paley is inviting us to contrast two probabilities. Suppose we define the 'predictive power' of a hypothesis in relation to a given body of evidence as the probability of the evidence given the hypothesis. We could write this as: $P(e/h)$, where h stands for the hypothesis, e for the evidence and $P(e/h)$ is read as 'the probability of the evidence given the hypothesis'. More exactly, we might suppose that the relevant probability is $P(e/h.k)$, to be read as 'the probability of the evidence given h and k', where k stands for 'background knowledge' – that is, whatever else we take ourselves to know about the world in addition to e. So $P(e/h.k)$ is the probability of e if h holds true, along with whatever else we take to be true. Drawing on this vocabulary, we can say that the first probability that Paley is inviting us to judge is the predictive power of the hypothesis of design, where e is the existence of a watch of the kind he describes in the passage above. He wants the reader to suppose that this probability is reasonably high, because we can see what purpose a designer might be aiming at in assembling such a structure. Then there is a second probability that he is inviting us to assess: the predictive power of the hypothesis of non-design, or of the set of hypotheses which make no appeal to the idea of design. This probability, he wants the reader to think, is relatively low, because of the delicate relationship between the organization of the watch's parts and their capacity to serve this purpose. Given the sensitive nature of this relationship, Paley is saying, it is not to be expected that this purpose-fulfilling arrangement would arise just anyhow. A precise set of causal preconditions will be required, and the non-design hypothesis has no account to give of why these conditions should obtain, he implies, because a non-designing system will be ignorant of the goal to be pursued, and a *fortiori* ignorant of the delicate relationship between the goal and the means which are fitted to bring it about.

Following the influential example of Richard Swinburne, a number of recent commentators have tried to capture the argumentativeforce of the argument from design by using the terms of Bayes's Theorem.

According to this theorem, the probability of a hypothesis, h, on certain evidence e is:

[1] $P(h/e.k) = \dfrac{P(h/k) \times P(e/h.k)}{P(e/k)}$

We can rewrite this relationship as:[11]

[2] $P(h/e.k) = \dfrac{\ldots\ldots\ldots P(h/k) \times P(e/h.k) \ldots\ldots\ldots}{[P(e/h.k) \times P(h/k)] + [P(e/not\text{-}h.k) \times P(not\text{-}h/k)]}$

$P(e/h.k)$ here is the predictive power of h; and $P(e/not\text{-}h.k)$ is the predictive power of the alternatives to h. So taking h to be the hypothesis of design, and e to be a structure of the kind that Paley describes in his example of the watch, then Paley's argument involves these two claims: we have reason to suppose that $P(e/h.k)$ is reasonably high, and that $P(e/not\text{-}h.k)$ is relatively low. And as we can see from the right-hand side of [2], other things being equal, the higher $P(e/h.k)$ and the lower $P(e/not\text{-}h.k)$, the higher will be the value of $P(h/e.k)$. So Paley's line of argument makes sense in broadly Bayesian terms. It also fits with common sense, of course: if a hypothesis h predicts some evidence with a reasonably high degree of probability, and if the set of alternatives to h does not do this, then the evidence at least confirms h, and may well give us reason to think that h is true.

We might ask ourselves: why does Paley not consider $P(h/k)$? The relevance of this probability is clear, both from Bayes's Theorem and commonsensically: even if a particular hypothesis h has a high predictive power, and even if the set of alternatives has a low predictive power, h might still fail to provide a good explanation of the evidence, because h might be intrinsically, that is, considered apart from the evidence, just too improbable. We know from his comments elsewhere that Paley thinks of the soul as a non-material substance.[12] So on his view of things, the postulation of a non-material designer does not involve any radical departure from our everyday ontology. (The designer will need to be non-material, we could say, because it will be 'external' to the world, as the source of its structure.) So it is perhaps partly for this reason that Paley does not consider the value of $P(h/k)$: he just assumes that the probability of the hypothesis of design on background knowledge cannot be too low, given what we know about the human mind, independently of what we know about the order of organisms.[13] It is also worth recalling his comment that: 'This mechanism being observed . . . the inference, we think, is inevitable, that the watch *must have had* a maker . . .' He clearly thinks that the inference he is presenting is pretty compelling: on his view, there is only one decent candidate explanation of the purpose-fulfilling mutual adjustment of the various parts of the mechanism, and in those circumstances, it is enough to refer to the relative predictive powers of the hypothesis of design and its alternatives. For even if P(h/k) were to be pretty low, h would remain the only viable explanation of the phenomena, given its decisive advantage in terms of predictive power.

So this is, I suggest, the logical structure of Paley's argument: his case turns on a judgement about the relative predictive powers of the design and non-design hypotheses, and it is buttressed, at least implicitly, by certain assumptions about the intrinsic probability of design. Thomas McPherson has tried to classify design arguments, by distinguishing between versions of the argument which appeal to what he calls 'design-A' and versions which appeal to 'design-B'. Design-A involves simply regularity in some respect, while design-B involves pur-pose.[14] Of course, an argument might combine these two varieties of design, and move from the observation of design-A to the claim that this is evidence of design-B. The strand of Paley's argument which is concerned with the predictive power of the design hypothesis is dealing with McPherson's design-B. If a structure can serve a purpose, then there are grounds for supposing that it is reasonably likely given the hypothesis of design. The strand of his argument which is addressed to the predictive power of the non-design hypothesis is dealing, I suggest, with design-A. We can see that the predictive power of the non-design hypothesis is quite low in relation to a structure such as that of the watch, Paley is urging, because we can see that this sort of structure involves a very particular arrangement of parts. The special character of this arrangement of the parts, their orderedness in this sense, is not directly observable on this account, since it has to do with the delicate relationship between the organization of the parts and their capacity to fulfil a purpose. So identifying this order requires us to make various counterfactual judgements, and to notice that if things had been arranged differently in various respects, then the purpose would not have been realized. So Paley's argument invites us to suppose that the identification of design-A can be relative to an understanding of design-B: we recognize that a structure is ordered in recognizing that it is precisely adjusted to the fulfillment of a purpose. And this is grounds, he is saying, for supposing that the structure is designed.

Applying the central argument

Having set out the watch example, Paley proceeds to argue, at least implicitly, that much the same considerations apply in a great host of cases drawn from observation of nature. He is interested above all in the structure of organisms. A stone, he notes, does not evidently serve any purpose; and it does not evidently display any kind of complex internal structure, let alone a structure that is delicately adjusted to the fulfillment of a purpose. So the watch argument will not be transferable to things such as stones, he thinks. By contrast, he urges, the structures of organisms seem to be very obviously purpose-fulfilling; and the purpose-securing capacity of these structures seems to stand in a delicate relationship to the organization and constitution of their parts. The centrepiece of Paley's approach to these matters, the example of organic structure to which he turns first, is the eye. In the case of the eye as in the case of a telescope, to take his preferred analogy at this juncture, there is a mechanism which serves the purpose of bringing an image into clear focus. And in each of these cases, the mechanism is delicately adjusted to the fulfillment of the purpose, because even small changes in the constitution of the parts, or in their relationship to one another, will frustrate the purpose. Indeed, Paley thinks that in some respects the eye is a more remarkable example of mechanism than the telescope. How, he wonders, is the eye to bring objects into clear focus when they lie at varying distances from itself? With a telescope, we can simply change the lens, or substitute one instrument for another; but these expedients will not serve in the case of the eye. Paley comments:

> whenever the eye is directed to a near object, three changes are produced in it at the same time, all severally contributing to the adjustment required. The cornea, or outermost coat of the eye, is rendered more round and prominent; the crystalline lens underneath is pushed forward; and the axis of vision, as the depth of the eye is called, is elongated. These changes in the eye vary its power over the rays of light in such a manner and degree as to produce exactly the effect which is

wanted, viz. the formation of an image *upon the retina*, whether the rays come to the eye in a state of divergency, which is the case when the object is near to the eye, or come parallel to one another, which is the case when the object is placed at a distance.[15]

Here we see the same line of argument as was evident in the case of the watch. First of all, Paley identifies a purpose: here, it is bringing an image into clear focus. Then he notes that the realization of this purpose requires a very precise disposition of the eye's parts, if this effect is to be secured for objects which stand at varying distances from it. Indeed Paley comments that this combination of alterations in the cornea, lens and axis of vision produces '*exactly* the effect which is wanted'. So the eye's parts do not produce merely an approximation to the desired effect, but precisely the effect required – which suggests that their arrangement stands in a highly sensitive relationship to that effect.

Characteristically, Paley is interested in the eyes of a range of creatures, not just in the human eye. The eyes of birds, he notes, are of particular interest, because here there is a special difficulty to be addressed: in order to feed, birds typically need to have a clear image of an object which lies close by, at the end of their beak; but at the same time, they need good distance vision, so they can see objects far removed from them when they are in flight. The consequence of these particular demands, Paley observes, is that the eyes of birds have a distinctive structure in two respects: they are encircled by a bony rim, which makes possible an increase of 'lateral pressure upon the orb'; and they have a special muscle which allows the lens to be retracted. 'By these means', he notes, 'the eyes of birds can pass from one extreme to another of their scale of adjustment, with more ease and readiness than the eyes of other animals.'[16]

Here we see how the eye can be geared up not just for seeing, but for the particular kind of seeing that is required to support a given mode of life. As Paley observes: 'by different species of animals the faculty we are describing is possessed, in degrees suited to the different range of vision which their mode of life, and of procuring their food, requires'.[17] So the purpose in question is highly particular: seeing *of the kind that is suited to such and such a mode of life*. And accordingly, the fulfillment of the purpose requires a correspondingly precise provision of parts and mutual adjustment of those parts.

A critic might wonder: isn't Paley begging the question in supposing that the eye, for example, exists *in order to* enable sight? Doesn't the purpose clause here simply presuppose the idea of a purposive agent; and shouldn't we speak more cautiously therefore of *apparent* purpose? But if we do speak of *apparent* purpose, then how is Paley to move convincingly to the idea of an actual purpose, which is to be ascribed to a transcendent designer? I don't think this charge is quite fair. As in the case of the watch, so here Paley is in effect inviting the reader to contrast two predictive powers. On the hypothesis of design, the structure of the eye is unsurprising, he is suggesting, because this structure can secure a purpose of the kind that can readily be ascribed to a designer, namely, the purpose of enabling sight. But Paley's argument also requires an assessment of the predictive power of the non-design hypothesis. And from the point of view of this hypothesis, we will of course have to speak of apparent, and not actual, purpose. So the possibility that the purpose here is only apparent is acknowledged in the structure of the argument: this is the perspective represented when we assess the predictive power of the non-design hypothesis. So on this point at least, there is no begging of the question.

Having begun with the example of the eye, Paley goes on to review an abundance of other cases, considering the bones, muscles and 'vessels' of human beings and a broad array of other creatures. His discussion extends to the stomachs of camels, the tongues of woodpeckers and many things besides![18] This wealth of detail, while fascinating in itself, is not directly relevant to our purposes – since we are concerned here with the logical structure of his argument, and this structure remains little changed, even when applied to such apparently diverse cases. So having set out the rudiments of Paley's argument, let's move now to consider its cogency. We can do this by examining in turn the force of Humean and Darwinian objections to his case.

The Humean critique of the design argument

In his *Dialogues Concerning Natural Religion*, Hume sets up a conversation between three principal characters: Cleanthes represents the argument from design, Demea propounds a more traditional form of religious apologetic, and in some ways a more traditional conception of God, while Philo assumes the role of the sceptic, and plays off his two inter-locutors against one another, showing that 'the' religious view of these matters is actually compounded of various not evidently compatible strands. Cleanthes's argument resembles Paley's in so far as it is built, like so many arguments of the period, around the machine analogy. His version of the argument rests upon this appeal:

> Look round the world, contemplate the whole and every part of it: you will find it to be nothing but one great machine, subdivided into an infinite number of lesser machines, which again admit of subdivisions to a degree beyond what human senses and faculties can trace and explain. All these various machines, and even their most minute parts, are adjusted to each other with an accuracy which ravishes into admiration all men who have ever contemplated them. The curious adapting of means to ends, throughout all nature, resembles exactly, though it much exceeds, the productions of human contrivance – of human design, thought, wisdom, and intelligence. Since therefore the effects resemble each other, we are led to infer, by all the rules of analogy, that the causes also resemble, and that the Author of nature is somewhat similar to the mind of man, though possessed of much larger faculties, proportioned to the grandeur of the work which he has executed.[19]

This argument resembles Paley's in speaking of the 'adapting of means to ends' (here is design-B), and in so far as it notes the 'accuracy' with which the parts of the structures of nature are 'adjusted to each other' (here is design-A). Again, if we are following Paley, the first of these points should lead us to think that the predictive power of the design hypothesis in relation to this body of evidence is reasonably high, while the second point should lead us to suppose that the predictive power of competing hypotheses is relatively low. However, Cleanthes's argument rather more emphatically than Paley's represents *the world* as a machine, whereas Paley's case is primarily concerned with the structure of individual organisms. More importantly, Cleanthes's argument is cast very explicitly in analogical terms. As he says: 'Since the effects resemble one another, we are led to infer by all the rules of analogy that the causes also resemble.'

Many commentators have thought that inferences of this analogical form are hazardous. As Stephen Davis observes:

> Obviously arguments from analogy can be weak. Notice this one: Jet planes and races horses are both fast; therefore, jet airplanes and race horses have similar

causes. What is lacking in these arguments is a reason to think that the cause must or might well be similar. The question is whether there is any other, more plausible explanation of the similar effects. Arguments from analogy are at their strongest where there is some reason to think that this is the case; some reason to think that alternative explanations will not wash. Thus . . . good arguments from analogy usually involve subarguments about which of the available explanations . . . is the *best* explanation.[20]

As Davis notes, Paley reasons analogically.[21] However, his case is importantly different from the kind of argument that features in this passage. As we have seen, Paley's argument turns on a judgement about the relative predictive power of the design and non-design hypotheses. If we look closely at the watch passage, we will find that Paley appeals to a judgement of this kind, and at no point does he introduce any kind of analogy. He does not, after all, compare the watch to anything else. A case of this kind is best construed, I suggest, not as an argument from analogy, but as an inference to the best explanation: Paley is arguing that the design hypothesis is the best explanation of a watch-like mechanism, because this hypothesis has a higher predictive power than does the set of alternative hypotheses. When Paley moves on, in later parts of the *Natural Theology*, to examine the structure of organisms, he does of course note that their structure is like that of the watch which he describes at the very beginning of this work. But his thought is not simply that organisms are like watches in some respects, rather as jet planes are like horses in certain respects, though not in others. Instead, the analogy consists in the fact that in the case of watches and organisms alike, there is a finely-tuned relationship between the parts of a thing and their capacity to serve a purpose. It is for this reason, according to Paley, that the predictive power of the design hypothesis exceeds that of its rivals in each case. So the analogy which he draws between organisms and watches does not really do any argumentative work: its role is just to draw our attention to the finely-tuned relationship between the parts of an organism and their capacity to serve a purpose; and it is this relationship which gives us reason to introduce the hypothesis of design.

As we have seen, Cleanthes's formulation of the design argument resembles Paley's later version of the argument. But Cleanthes does not present in any detail the idea that the relative predictive power of the design and non-design hypotheses holds the key to the argumentative force of the design hypothesis. So his case is more easily construed as a simple argument from analogy, which moves from the fact that we have seen watches being designed, and the fact that organisms resemble watches in some respects, to the claim that organisms are designed. To this extent, Cleanthes's version of the design argument is more vulnerable to the sort of difficulty that Davis notes.

In the *Dialogues*, Philo goes on to exploit precisely these weaknesses. He argues for example that Cleanthes's analogical mode of argument will issue in a theologically defective conception of the designer's nature. After all, if the argument turns on the idea that the world is to be explained in terms of design because it is like (here is the analogy) the kinds of thing that you and I make, then should we not conclude that any designer of the world will be rather like you and me? Philo goes so far as to urge: 'Why not become a perfect anthropomorphite? Why not assert the deity or deities to be corporeal, and to have eyes, a nose, mouth, ears, etc.?'[22] This objection is not so telling if we construe the design argument as an inference to the best explanation. If it is understood in this way, then the argument supports only the conclusion that certain features of the world are best explained in terms of purposive (rather than, more exactly, human-like) agency. And the idea of purposive agency does not of itself entail or otherwise imply the idea of anthropomorphic agency. In fact, if such an entailment were to hold, then *all* standard forms of theism would issue in anthropomorphism, not just those which derive from the design argument – since all these views involve the idea of a God who acts purposefully.

There is no direct evidence from the *Natural Theology* that Paley had read Hume's *Dialogues*: he does not cite Hume and there are no direct allusions to his work. However, immediately after the passage where he sets down the example of the watch, Paley reviews various possible objections to his case, and some of these objections have a decidedly Humean feel. We might plausibly speculate that Humean kinds of objection were at any rate 'in the air', and that Paley was aware of them to this extent. For example, he remarks: 'Nor would it, I apprehend, weaken the conclusion, that we had never seen a watch made'.[23] This recalls Philo's objection in the *Dialogues* that to know that the world is designed 'it were requisite that we had experience of the origin of worlds'. Paley's brisk dismissal of this objection points again to the fact that his argument does not have this structure: we know that organisms are designed, because they are like watches in certain respects, and we know that watches are designed *from observation*.

> Another of Philo's objections runs as follows:

> A tree bestows order and organization on that tree which springs from it, without knowing the order; an animal in the same manner on its offspring . . . To say that all this order in animals and vegetables proceeds ultimately from design is begging the question.[24]

Again, Paley seems familiar with the objection and to have prepared a response. In reply to this sort of point, he raises the possibility that the watch found on the heath might turn out to have 'the unexpected property of producing, in the course of its movement, another watch like itself . . .'[25] And he notes that such a discovery would hardly undermine the supposition of design. On the contrary: 'The first effect would be to increase [the observer's] admiration of the contrivance, and his conviction of the consummate skill of the contriver'.

This issue brings us rather directly to the evolutionary case against Paley. So let us consider these matters next, before proceeding to a closer examination of this objection.

The Darwinian critique of the design argument

I have been arguing that at least some of Hume's many objections to the design argument fail to count against Paley's version of the argument. However, it might seem that Paley's case is rather obviously susceptible to a Darwinian kind of objection. After all, does he not say, again and again, that the purpose-fulfilling character of organic structures consists in the fact that they enable the organism to thrive according to the demands of its particular mode of life? As we have seen, he understands the special properties of birds' eyes in these terms, citing their role in enabling birds to locate food. My own favourite example concerns the relationship between a mole's feet and its eyes: given its feet, this creature needs eyes that are fitted to a subterranean mode of life, and vice versa![26] Of course, from a Darwinian point of view, there is another account altogether of why we find this sort of 'relation', as Paley terms it, between the parts of an organism and its environment.

On a Darwinian view, creatures which do not exhibit such a fit will be unable to complete for scarce resources, and this sufficiently explains why there are no such creatures to be found.

Fascinatingly, at one point in the *Natural Theology*, Paley comes within a hair's breadth of a Darwinian kind of perspective upon adaptedness. In the following passage, he is considering another objection which he may have encountered, even if only rather indirectly, through Hume. In the *Dialogues*, Philo introduces the 'Epicurean hypothesis', which he glosses as the idea that 'it must happen, in an eternal duration, that every possible order [of things] or position must be tried an infinite number of times'. And he asks: why should the order we observe not have resulted from some such shuffling of bits of matter, bearing in mind that an order 'when once established, supports itself for many ages if not to eternity'?[27] In a similar vein, Paley considers this possibility: perhaps 'every organized body which we see' has resulted from 'the lapse of infinite ages', 'millions of other bodily forms and other species having perished, being by the defect of their constitution incapable of preservation, or of continuance by generation'. But he rejects this supposition, noting that:

> no such experiments are going on at present . . . Nor are there any appearances to support an opinion, that every possible combination of vegetable or animal structure has formerly been tried. Multitudes of conformations, both of vegetables and animals, may be conceived capable of existence and succession, which yet do not exist.[28]

Paley first claims here that no new creaturely types are emerging in the present. Of course, drawing on the work of Darwin and his successors, we must now say that we have an abundance of evidence for such variation, in the present as in the past. He then says that even if creaturely types have varied, this would still not account for the data. But crucially, the counter-proposal to his own position which he is considering here has this conjunctive form: [i] *all* possible creaturely types have been tried; and [ii] the creaturely types we observe are adapted to their environments because adaptation is a precondition of survival and reproduction. Paley rejects this conjunctive hypothesis, reasoning that creatures such as unicorns seem to be perfectly viable, yet lack existence. But he fails to consider a more modest version of this proposal, which substitutes for [i] this claim: [iii] *a finite set* of creaturely types has been tried. This more modest hypothesis seems to match Darwin's picture of the world, and by contrast with the proposal which Paley is examining, this hypothesis is entirely consistent with the non-existence of creatures such as unicorns.

Should we conclude that Paley has underestimated the predictive power of the non-design hypothesis, by failing to recognize that finite variation plus selection can account for the fit between organisms and the demands of their environment? In other words, is the problem that Paley has failed to anticipate Darwin? This conclusion would be too quick, for a number of reasons. Let's return first of all to the idea of a self-reproducing watch. Paley devotes a chapter of the *Natural Theology* to the question of 'the succession of plants and animals'.[29] He examines the generative powers of various kinds of plant and animal, and he finds that succession always depends upon mechanism: in each case, there is a delicate relationship between relevant parts of the organism and its capacity to produce more of its kind. Paley is surely right about this to this extent: the sexual organs of an animal, for example, surely present as plausible an instance of purposive fine-tuning as does the eye. Of course, Paley did not intend these remarks as a rebuttal of a Darwinian-style objection to the design argument. He had not even conceived of such an objection. But these comments are of interest for two reasons. First, they direct our attention again to the non-analogical character of his argument. In so far as they reproduce themselves, organisms are *not* like watches as we know them – but this disanalogy does not perturb Paley, because, once again, his case is not at root an argument from analogy. And second, Paley's suggestion that design provides the best explanation of the reproductive powers of plants and animals cannot be trumped by some Darwinian counter-explanation, because Darwinian forms of explanation rest on the idea of reproduction with variation, so ultimately *presuppose* the existence of creatures with a capacity to reproduce. As Anthony Kenny has remarked, 'the mechanisms of evolutionary pressure and selection . . . cannot explain the existence of breeding populations, since that is one of the principles of evolutionary explanation'.[30] So in at least one respect, Paley's version of the design argument turns out to be invulnerable to a Darwinian kind of counter-proposal – for logical reasons, and not just because of contingent gaps in our understanding.

Modern proponents of the design argument have adopted various strategies to evade the force of the Darwinian critique of the argument. One strategy has been to identify features of the world which are pre-supposed in Darwinian kinds of explanation. Pressing the question 'why should there by any breeding populations in the first place?' provides one instance of this sort of strategy. Another example of this approach involves the thought that Darwinian evolution requires a precise set of planetary or cosmological conditions, and that the hypothesis of design is the best predictor of these conditions. Paley's work anticipates the modern debate on this point too. For instance, he argues at some length that the 'elements' of air, fire, water and light are present in just the form and degree that is required for the existence of life. Here is one of his examples: 'Were it not for the presence of heat, or of a certain degree of it, all fluids would be frozen. The ocean itself would be a quarry of ice; universal nature stiff and dead'.[31] Of course, we know as Paley did not that our own planet was once in precisely this condition. Similarly, he notes that 'if a planet once set off revolving upon any other than its shortest, or one of its longest axes, the poles on its surface would keep perpetually changing, and it never would attain a perman-ent axis of rotation'.[32] Again, no Darwinian story of the evolution of species could unfold under these conditions, presumably, because the environment of such a planet would be too unstable to support life of any complexity.

F. R. Tennant has argued similarly that the design argument should appeal to the life-enabling character of our planet. In fact, he distin-guishes this sort of approach from 'the Paleyan type of teleology which relied on particular organic adaptations . . .' Evidently, this is a little unfair to Paley, since Paley's account already has this broader focus.[33] More recently, the so-called 'fine-tuning' argument has extended this sort of strategy, by proposing that the character of the cosmos at the time of the Big Bang (for instance, its expansion rate, and the ratio of hydrogen to helium) was delicately related to the possibility of life's development.[34] This argument is clearly of the same type as Paley's case from the sensitive relationship between the axis of rotation of a planet and its consistency with life. Here again the modern literature is able to draw on recent advances in the sciences, but in fundamental conception its approach is little different from Paley's.

It is striking that Paley himself was rather uneasy about grounding a design argument in facts about the elements or astronomical phenomena, noting that we do not know enough about the elements or, for example, the planets to understand their internal structure.[35] But his procedure in these cases confirms what is anyway evident: his version of the design argument is not in the narrow sense 'mechanical'. Rather, his case depends on showing how the realisation of a given purpose is sensitively related to the values which are assumed by a number of independent variables, and it does not matter much whether these variables concern the shape or composition of the eye, or the axis of rotation of a planet.

So in the post-Darwinian era, some proponents of design have appealed to features of the world which are presupposed by, rather than possibly explained by, the processes described by Darwin. There is one other broadly defined response to Darwinism in the modern literature. This approach aims to identify properties of organisms which, while not presupposed by a Darwinian kind of explanation, lie beyond its reach even so, because they confer, whether directly or indirectly, no adaptive advantage. Tennant notes, for example, how the natural world is 'saturated' with beauty, despite the fact that 'in the organic world aesthetic pleasingness of colour, etc., seems to possess survival-value on but a limited scale, and then is not to be identified with the complex and intellectualized aesthetic sentiments of humanity, which apparently have no survival-value'.[36] More recently, 'intelligent design' arguments have popularized this sort of approach, by proposing that certain organisms exhibit 'irreducible complexity'.[37] On this view, the parts of some organisms confer an evolutionary benefit only when they exist in combination. This makes it hard, so the argument goes, to see how such structures could have emerged incrementally, following the standard evolutionary story. It is noteworthy that Paley also produces arguments which share the logical form of this second style of response to Darwin, although once again some of his data may be judged unreliable by the standards of modern science. For instance, he draws attention to the beauty of certain flowers, and notes that this property appears to be 'independent . . . of the wants and utilities of the plant', and therefore cannot be explained in those terms.[38] Or again, he proposes that the epiglottis could not have been produced 'in a succession of

generations' by means of a process of incremental development –
because 'the animal could not live . . . either without it, or with it in a
half-formed state'.[39]

Concluding remarks

How forceful, then, is Paley's version of the design argument? As
we have seen, his case depends upon a judgement about the relative
predictive power of the design hypothesis and rival hypotheses. From
our modern vantage point, it seems that he has *under*estimated the
predictive power of the non-design hypothesis, because he did not
fully anticipate Darwin's account of the fit between creatures and their
environments. For this reason, some of his examples will fail to convince
a modern readership. However, Paley did see that any explanation of
adaptedness which appeals to reproduction (as Darwinian arguments do)
will leave at least one important example of adaptedness unexplained.
And he did see that any account of adaptedness which cites its survival-
value will have to reckon with the existence of traits and structures
which apparently confer no survival-value, or which could not evidently
have been produced by a succession of steps each of which confers
some adaptive advantage. He also saw that the existence of creatures
which are adapted to their local environments depends upon the life-
friendliness of a broader planetary and cosmological context, and that
the design hypothesis may offer our best explanation of this context.
Lastly, because he introduces the postulate of design as the best
explanation of the data, rather than relying on any crude appeal to
analogy, Paley's case is not so vulnerable to Humean kinds of objection
as many have thought.

   In Paley's view, we should have recourse to the idea of design whenever
we find a finely-tuned relationship between a number independent
variables and the fulfillment of a purpose. In such cases, he says, rather
confidently, that 'there must have existed . . . an artificer or artificers'.[40]
More cautiously, we might say that in such cases there is a reason to
speak of design, but a reason which can be defeated, as Darwin's work
showed for some of Paley's own examples. Even so, Paley's case for
design was surely worth heeding in his own day, in spite of Hume; and

with regard to its logical form, it is surely still worth heeding today, in spite of Darwin.

Notes

1 Robert Hurlbutt III, *Hume, Newton and the Design Argument*, 136, my emphasis.
2 Richard Dawkins, *The Blind Watchmaker*, 6.
3 James E. Crimmins, 'Paley, William', *Oxford Dictionary of National Biography*, Vol. 42, 446.
4 N. Barlow, ed., *The Autobiography of Charles Darwin* (1958), 59, reproduced in the *Oxford Dictionary of National Biography*, 451.
5 See 'Anaxagoras', in Jonathan Barnes, *Early Greek Philosophy*.
6 See John Dillenberger, 'The Apologetic Defence of Christianity', in C. A. Russell, ed., *Science and Religious Belief: A Selection of Recent Historical Studies*, 183–5.
7 Charles Raven, *Natural Religion and Christian Theology*, 173.
8 *Dictionary of National Biography*, 449.
9 See this comment of Philo: 'The world plainly resembles more an animal or vegetable than it does a watch . . .': *Dialogues Concerning Natural Religion*, Part VII, 47.
10 William Paley, *Natural Theology; or Evidences of the Existence and Attributes of the Deity, Collected from the Appearances of Nature*, Vol. I, 1–4.
11 Swinburne gives this expansion in *The Existence of God*, 2nd edition, 72.
12 See for example his sermon on 'The Being of God Demonstrated in the Works of Creation', in *The Works of William Paley D.D.*, Vol. VI, XXXIII, Part II, 415.
13 Contrast Paley's stance on this issue with that of John Mackie: see *The Miracle of Theism: Arguments for and Against the Existence of God*, 149. As Swinburne has noted in his reply to Mackie on this point, we need to be careful not to include within k aspects of the world which are being subsumed under e. See *The Existence of God*, revised edition, 293–4.
14 Thomas McPherson, *The Argument from Design*, 8.
15 *Natural Theology*, Vol. I, 26.
16 *Natural Theology*, Vol. I, 28–30.
17 *Natural Theology*, Vol. I, 28.
18 These examples can be found in *Natural Theology*, Vol. II, 9–12.
19 *Dialogues*, Part II, 17.
20 Stephen T. Davis, *God, Reason and the Theistic Proofs*, 1997, 99–100.
21 *God, Reason and the Theistic Proofs*, 99.
22 *Dialogues*, Part V, 40.

23 *Natural Theology*, Vol. I, 4.

24 *Dialogues*, Part VII, 50.

25 *Natural Theology*, Vol. I, 8.

26 *Natural Theology*, Vol. II, 33–4.

27 *Dialogues*, 32–3.

28 *Natural Theology*, Vol. I, 62–3.

29 *Natural Theology*, Vol. I, Chapter IV, 49–54.

30 Anthony Kenny, *Reason and Religion: Essays in Philosophical Theology*, 78.

31 *Natural Theology*, Vol. II, 143.

32 *Natural Theology*, Vol. II, 154–155.

33 F. R. Tennant, *Philosophical Theology*, Vol. II, 85.

34 See for example John Leslie's defence of the argument in *Universes*.

35 He notes for example that it is difficult to take the character of the heavenly bodies as evidence for design because they 'do not, except perhaps in the instance of Saturn's ring, present themselves to our observation as compounded of any parts at all . . . They do not come within our mechanics': *Natural Theology*, Vol. II, 147.

36 *Philosophical Theology*, Vol. II, 91–2.

37 See for example Neil Manson, ed., *God and Design: The Teleological Argument and Modern Science*, Part IV, and Robert Stewart, ed., *Intelligent Design: William A. Dembski & Michael Ruse in Dialogue*.

38 *Natural Theology*, Vol. I, 204–5.

39 *Natural Theology*, Vol. I, 183.

40 This is the form of words he uses in his discussion of the watch.

Bibliography

Barnes, Jonathan. *Early Greek Philosophy* (Harmondsworth: Penguin, 1987).

Crimmins, James E., 'Paley, William'. *Oxford Dictionary of National Biography*, (ed.) H. C. G. Matthew and B. Harrison (Oxford: Oxford University Press, 2004), Vol. 42, 445–51.

Davis, Stephen T. *God, Reason and the Theistic Proofs* (Edinburgh: Edinburgh University Press, 1997).

Dawkins, Richard. *The Blind Watchmaker* (London: Penguin, 1988).

Dillenberger, John. 'The Apologetic Defence of Christianity', in C. A. Russell, (ed.) *Science and Religious Belief: A Selection of Recent Historical Studies* (Sevenoaks: Open University Press, 1973), 170–94.

Hume, David. *Dialogues Concerning Natural Religion*, (ed.) Henry Aiken (New York: Hafner Publishing Company, 1959).

Hurlbutt III, Robert. *Hume, Newton and the Design Argument* (Lincoln, NE: University of Nebraska Press, 1965).

Kenny, Anthony. *Reason and Religion: Essays in Philosophical Theology* (Oxford: Blackwell, 1987).

Leslie, John. *Universes* (London: Routledge, 1989).

Mackie, John. *The Miracle of Theism: Arguments for and Against the Existence of God* (Oxford: Oxford University Press, 1982).

Manson, Neil. (ed.) *God and Design: The Teleological Argument and Modern Science* (London: Routledge, 2003).

McPherson, Thomas. *The Argument from Design* (London: Macmillan, 1972).

Paley, William. *Natural Theology; or Evidences of the Existence and Attributes of the Deity, Collected from the Appearances of Nature* (Oxford: J. Vincent, 2nd edition, 1828).

Paley, William. *The Works of William Paley D. D., with Additional Sermons and a Corrected Account of the Life and Writings of the Author: A New Edition.* (ed.) Edmund Paley (London: C. and J. Rivington et al 1825).

Raven, Charles. *Natural Religion and Christian Theology* (Cambridge: Cambridge University Press, 1953).

Stewart, Robert. (ed.) *Intelligent Design: William A. Dembski & Michael Ruse in Dialogue* (Minneapolis: Fortress, 2007).

Swinburne, Richard. *The Existence of God* (Oxford: Oxford University Press, revised edition, 1991; 2nd edition, 2004).

Tennant, F. R. *Philosophical Theology*, Vol. II, *The World, the Soul and God* (Cambridge: Cambridge University Press, 1956; 1st edition, 1928).

CHAPTER 6

KANT AND THE MORAL ARGUMENT
Peter Byrne

Introduction[1]

Many different arguments for the existence of God can be and have been styled 'moral arguments'. All start from premises about morality or the moral life of human beings. All support belief in, or acceptance of, the existence of something like the God of standard theism.[2] Within this broad family of arguments a distinction must be drawn between evidential and non-evidential forms of moral argument.[3] Evidential forms of the moral argument are on a par with standard arguments in natural theology. They cite alleged facts about morality or the moral life that are claimed to be evident to human experience. And they argue that such facts entail or are best explained by the hypothesis that there is a God with the attributes traditionally ascribed to him. Non-evidential arguments take us away from the patterns of argument typical of natural theology. They deal in our ends and motives. These variants on the moral argument for God's existence describe some end that the moral life commits us to (such as the attainment of the perfect good) and contend that this end cannot be rationally pursued unless God as traditionally defined is postulated. A typical aim of such non-evidential, moral arguments is that of showing that commitment to the moral life is irrational unless it is accompanied by acceptance of the claim that there is a God.

Kant is one of the most important developers and defenders of the moral argument. It is notable that his favoured versions of the moral argument are of the non-evidential type. This relates to an important aspect of his philosophy of religion: his rejection of natural theology. Kant has recourse to the moral argument (non-evidential) after concluding that the traditional project of natural theology fails. It must fail for Kant because it over-steps the boundaries that surround human cognition. It is the aim of Kant's Critical Philosophy (that is, the metaphysics and theory of knowledge expounded in the *Critique of Pure Reason* of 1781 and in later works) to set such limits. These boundaries prevent us having knowledge of the existence of an entity such as God who transcends all possible human experience. This means that reason, in one sense, is unable to lead the human mind to embrace God's existence. Reason in its theoretical mode, whereby it seeks to add to and systematise our knowledge of facts, cannot lead to God. This is why Kant states in the Preface to the 2nd edition of the *Critique of Pure Reason* 'Therefore I had to deny *knowledge* in order to make room for *faith*.'[4] This last remark is not what it seems. Kant is not saying that acceptance of God's existence comes about through a non-rational leap or decision. It is, rather, the outcome of reason, but of practical reason and not theoretical reason. What the moral argument (aided by other arguments that flow from the need for reason to orient itself in the world) does is ground a pure '*rational faith*' in God.[5] 'Faith' here translates *Glaube* and can equally be rendered as 'belief'. It does not have the connotations of wilful belief beyond or despite the evidence that attach to the f-word in English. Kant is a paid-up religious rationalist. It is merely that it is reason in its practical mode, relying largely on a non-evidential moral argument, which leads the human mind to God.

Evidential moral arguments

Our treatment of evidential moral arguments must be highly selective. Many arguments of this type start from the features of morality that are debated in meta-ethics.[6] One such feature is the alleged fact of ethical normativity. Human beings are aware of actions as being right and wrong, obligatory and forbidden. Such awareness carries with it the thought that they are 'bound' to do some things and bound to avoid doing others. Moral qualities have a bindingness attached to them shown in the force of the moral 'ought' and the moral 'must'. If I make a promise, the promise creates (*ceteris paribus*) an obligation to deliver what is promised. The normative fact is, first, not dependent on my own goals and ends and, second, possessed of a universal force. The fact that I am bound by the normative truth 'do what you promised' does not hold because I have ends which I cannot achieve unless I fulfil the promise. The imperative is not what Kant styled a 'hypothetical' one. It is rather 'categorical'. It binds no matter what my particular goals are.[7] That is linked to its universal dimension. I have an obligation to deliver what I promised, because anyone who makes a promise thereby (*ceteris paribus*) obligates him- or herself. The obligation created by the promise holds independent of my particular goals because it reflects a universal rule, holding at all times and places and applying to any human being as such.

Promise-making, and other forms of moral relation, seem to create a peculiar class of fact in the world. They are objective facts, holding regardless of human beings' opinions. They are also normative facts, facts to which a special kind of categorical bindingness attaches. What is the best explanation of such facts? Some answer: 'God'. Thus we find in a well-known survey or moral arguments by Robert Adams[8] the advocacy of this argument:

1. Moral facts exist.
2. Moral facts have the properties of being objective and non-natural.
3. The best explanation of there being objective and non-natural moral facts is provided by theism.
4. Therefore the existence of moral facts provides good grounds for thinking theism is true.

Premise (1) of this argument has been introduced already. So has the first claim in premise (2). The second claim therein – that moral facts are non-natural – expresses Adams' belief that moral facts that 'cannot be stated entirely in the language of physics, chemistry, biology, and human or animal psychology'.[9] If we merely had the language of the sciences to hand, then we could not account for the existence of facts with the peculiar quality of bindingness found behind categorical moral truths. Notice a contrast in this regard between moral facts and other apparent normative facts. The fact that the traffic light stands at red means that I must stop my car on approaching it. But the bindingness of the light's being red is dependent on a complex of human conventions, decisions and beliefs. Because of that it is not objective in the relevant sense and we can easily imagine it being otherwise. There is no reason whatsoever why the convention in traffic laws should not have been 'Green for stop, amber for get ready, red for go'. But, it is alleged, this does not make sense in relation to moral facts.

Premise (3) of Adams' argument invites us to accept that only a supernatural explanation of moral facts will do. What we need is a source of the norms that make such facts as 'You ought not to steal John's car', 'You owe Jennie £5' obtain. These will be the appropriate norms: 'Promises create obligations, *ceteris paribus*', 'One ought not to steal, (*ceteris paribus*)'. God as the source of these norms best fits the bill. He would be a non-conventional and objective source, establishing them quite independent of human desires and decisions; and He would give them binding authority, by virtue of his legitimate power over the minds and wills of human beings. This last point tacitly refers us to a main feature of so-called divine command theories of ethics, the contention that facts about our moral obligations obtain in virtue of divinely-given norms for human conduct that are backed by the providential power of God, who will reward and punish human beings in this life and the next.

As an argument for the best explanation for an alleged fact of human experience, this sample evidential moral argument faces a range of standard replies. In relation to a natural theological argument to God as the best explanation of some fact of human experience, three important strategies are open to the atheistic or agnostic philosopher: (1) deny the existence of the alleged fact from which the argument starts; (2) contend that it can be explained without appeal to God; (3) urge that God would not be a good explanation for it.

Replies (1) and (2) take us in to the territory of meta-ethics. One option in meta-ethics consists of irrealism. Irrealism comes in different forms, but common to them all is the assertion that moral judgements do not correspond to human-independent moral facts. A view that takes moral judgements to be akin to expressions of attitude or emotion will have this consequence; so will one that proposes an error-theory for moral judgements. Forms of irrealism will admit that moral judgements *appear* to be truth-valued, but such theories will employ resources to explain away this appearance as a naturally occurring illusion. It should be noted that the very fact that the argument is made that realism in meta-ethics has to rest on a supernatural world-view is a powerful motive for many thinkers to explain away the appearance of there being objective moral facts. Reply (2) has life because meta-ethics contains theories that accept as a given that moral judgements are true or false in virtue of their relation to objective facts, but which steer clear of a supernaturalist grounding of these facts. One set of such theories are naturalistic. Meta-ethical theories of this kind deny the second half of premise (2) of Adams' moral argument. They assert that moral facts can be a function of natural facts. Another set of meta-ethical theories offer non-naturalist interpretations of moral facts, but not supernaturalist ones. Non-naturalist theories agree with premise (2): Moral facts have the properties of being objective and non-natural. But they think that non-natural moral facts are *sui generis*, non-reducible to either natural facts or supernatural facts about the will of a transcendent creator.[10]

Rehearsing these facts about the state of play in meta-ethics establishes of itself an important point about evidential moral arguments for God's existence of the kind considered: they cannot succeed as proofs of theism. The reason for this is that rival, non-theistic, meta-ethical theories remain live options in philosophy. Retreat to one or other of them allows a non-theistic thinker to wriggle out of the conclusion that God is the best explanation of apparent facts about the nature or moral judgements.

The premise (3) assertion that God is the best explanation of moral normativity can be challenged in other ways than by pressing the claims of non-supernatural accounts of the foundations to ethics. Critics of moral arguments of the kind offered by Adams also directly attack the explanatory power of theism in this regard. As noted already, it is the role of God as the commander of the moral law that is alleged to provide an explanation of the bindingness of moral facts. Criticisms of divine command theories of ethics are legion. One line of criticism is worth picking out because it ties in neatly with a theme in Kant's ethics.

At the heart of Adams' premise (3) are claims of this kind:

The mere fact that I promised to do so-and-so cannot oblige me to do so unless there is a divine command that promises ought to be kept.

The mere fact that doing so-and-so would cause great pain to another cannot oblige me not to do it unless there is a divine command that one should not harm others.

Facts about the world cannot bring binding obligations of this kind into being; only divine commands can do this. But how can divine commands create obligations? It seems as if a divine command can create an obligation to do something only if a principle of the following kind is true:

> For any action and any agent, if God commands that agent to do that action, then the agent is obliged to do that action.

But this principle at the heart of divine command theories of ethics seems to be its true Achilles' heel. For it is both a substantive principle of obligation and not something that can depend on divine commands for its truth – it is rather presupposed by the thought that divine commands create obligations. So for divine commands to create obligations, not all obligations can be created by divine commands.[11] If we are to avoid infinite regress, it appears at least one fact must be intrinsically obligating.

The notion of a fact that, once apprehended, is seen to be intrinsically obligating seems utterly mysterious at first sight. But we recognize such facts in other areas of thought. If we see that two of our beliefs are contradictory, then we see that we ought to modify or abandon at least one of them. The 'norm of reason' that we ought not to hold contradictory beliefs is intrinsically authoritative. It does not depend on the commands of a Great Logician in the sky. Once we start to reflect on the very broad range of norms related to correct inferences and the appropriate justification of beliefs, then we see that there is a long list of such norms we sign up to in our logical and epistemological reflections.

One strand in meta-ethics builds upon the acknowledgement of norms of reason to suggest that moral norms are analogous to such norms: intrinsically motivating, authoritative and apprehended by rational reflection and intuition – in the same way that logical and epistemic norms are apprehended. This strand of ethical theory is non-naturalist (since it does not reduce moral facts and qualities to natural ones), but not supernaturalist.[12] An important corollary attaches to this approach to the foundations of ethics: it entails the claim that reason can of itself be practical. Reason can be practical of itself if the rational apprehension of that which is good and/or right provides a sufficient motive for action. What is the alternative to reason's being practical of itself? It is the view, sometimes known as 'reasons internalism', that no apprehension of a good or of a norm can move the will to act unless what is apprehended connects with a prior, existing motive (such as: an interest, a desire or an aim) of the agent. David Hume's declaration of the impotence of human reason, in his *Treatise of Human Nature*, is an archetypal expression of this opinion

> Since morals, therefore, have an influence on the actions and affections, it follows, that they cannot be deriv'd from reason; and that because reason alone, as we have already prov'd, can never have any such influence. Morals excite passions, and produce or prevent actions. Reason of itself is utterly impotent in this particular. The rules of morality, therefore, are not conclusions of our reason.[13]

It is an axiom of Kant's Critical moral philosophy, as set out in the *Groundwork of the Metaphysics of Morals* (1785) and the *Critique of Practical Reason* (1788), that Hume's position on the impotence of reason is the reverse of the truth. So far as the laws of morality are concerned, reason is of itself practical. 'Reason determines the will in a practical law immediately'.[14] 'Immediately' means: without the mediation of one of Hume's 'passions' or of one of the agent's prior aims or motives. The possession by human beings of the faculty of reason entails that they can rise above a merely physical existence. That shows them to be in part members of an 'intelligible world'. The possession of reason is thereby the key to freedom for Kant. As members of the physical world, the world disclosed by sense-experience, our thoughts and actions are part of the natural, causal process. But as creatures of reason we can be held to be responsible for our actions insofar as reason is able to move us directly to obey our moral duties. We may not plead that we had no choice if we fall short of them and thereby violate the norms of right. In these important respects, many commentators see an important contrast between Kant's Critical and pre-Critical ethics. Prior to his Critical phase, Kant for some time held the view that while reason presented us with a knowledge of our duties, morality also had to engage with our feelings and affections if such knowledge was to move us to action.[15] With his mature view that the rational apprehension of moral norms brings with them a sense of their bindingness, it appears that Kant cannot endorse those evidential forms of a moral argument for God's existence that appeal to divine will to give moral norms authority. They are intrinsically binding. He cannot say that the moral law has its author in God. The moral law has no author for Kant. The moral law is unlike a positive law that can be created through some agent's will – which is just what it would be if a crude version of the divine command theory of ethics were true.[16]

A mark of Kant's departure from the outlook which produces the kind of evidential moral argument we have discussed is his assertion that the moral law applies to all rational beings. Indeed, it applies to God. God, therefore, stands under the moral law; thus his will must be logically posterior to it and not prior. Though it should be noted that God, as a perfectly rational and holy being, never feels the moral law as a constraint, as a command; he simply acts in accordance with it.[17]

For all these reasons, Kant's own moral argument must be of a very different stripe from that of Adams'.

Kant's non-evidential moral argument

At a number of places in his Critical writings Kant offers a moral argument for God whose essence can be set out as follows:

1. It is rationally and morally necessary to attain the highest good (perfect happiness arising out of complete virtue).
2. What we are obliged to attain, it must be possible for us to attain.
3. Attaining the highest good is only possible if natural order and causality are part of an overarching moral order and moral causality.
4. Moral order and moral causality can only be conceived to be possible if we postulate a God as their moral source.

The most famous exposition of the above is to be found in the *Critique of Practical Reason*.[18] The remainder of this chapter is devoted to analysis and criticism of this argument under a number of key heads.

The nature of the argument and the force of its conclusion
The argument is about the rationality of living the moral life, that is a life governed by the attempt to be obedient to the moral law so far is humanly possible. Such a life is irrational unless we can conceive that its necessary goal, the highest good, is possible of attainment. This by itself indicates that it is not the purpose of the argument to offer us evidence

that makes the proposition 'There is a God' certain or even more probable. Further to this, Kant presents his 'moral proof' as one that mandates the use of God as a 'postulate' of practical reason. Postulation is related to assumption and faith. Kant states: 'Therefore, the highest good in the world is only possible insofar as a supreme cause of nature is assumed, which has a causality corresponding to the moral disposition'.[19] The argument leads to pure rational faith (Glaube) in God.[20] Kant makes it plain in a number of places that Glaube in God is not the kind of thing that requires, or can have, evidence behind it. He says there is a scale of assent based on evidence that goes from opinion at one end to knowledge at the other. Opinion involves taking something to be true in a hesitant fashion and where the proposition in question is backed by little evidence. Knowledge involves taking something to be true with strong conviction and where there are grounds that make it objectively certain. Opinion and knowledge are on the same scale. The one can be transformed into the other by the awareness of the addition or deletion of evidence, as appropriate. But faith is simply not on this scale. It is a taking-to-be-true that is wholehearted, but where the question of evidence does not arise because the acceptance of the relevant proposition is based on the perceived demands of our practical reason.[21] What Kant has in mind by 'faith' is best reconstructed by seeing it as a version of what in contemporary epistemology is called 'acceptance'. Whereas belief is an involuntary state that just comes to the subject upon her awareness of reasons, evidence, argument and the like, acceptance is the voluntary taking on a positive attitude towards a proposition. It is a positive attitude because the accepter assumes the truth of the proposition in further theorizing and in formulating policies of action. In acceptance we do this voluntarily and in the absence of clear evidence that makes us think the proposition is true, as when we accept something for the sake of argument or as a working assumption.[22]

Kant's moral argument tells us that, for the sake of supporting our commitment to the necessary end of the moral life (the attainment of the highest good), we must accept that there is a God. That acceptance enables us to think and act on the assumption that, despite appearances, the doing of right acts because they are right, and the acquisition of a perfected disposition to behave thus, will be the means of securing perfect happiness. This means accepting that there is a moral order to reality. Though consequent well-being and misery appear to have no law-like connection to the morality of our actions, if we accept that there is a God with the traditional attributes, then we can be assured that they will have – in the fullness of time.

As well as not producing straightforward belief in God, there is another limitation in the conclusion of Kant's argument. In Kant's statements of the moral proof in his major works he makes it plain that it is not really a proof. It does not lead to the conclusion that it is certain there is a God, but only to the conclusion that *I* am certain that there is a God.[23] It is specifically characterized as 'a subjective argument' in the third *Critique* a verdict that follows this account of its force:

> This moral argument is not meant to offer any *objectively* valid proof of the existence of God, nor meant to prove to the sceptic that there is a God; rather it is meant to show him that he *must adopt* the assumption of this proposition among the maxims of his practical reason if his moral thinking is to be consistent. – Thus it is also not intended to affirm: it is necessary *for morality* that the happiness of all rational beings in the world in accordance with their morality be assumed; but rather it is necessary *through it* [morality]. Thereby it is a sufficient, *subjective* argument for moral beings.[24]

The subjective force of the argument is highlighted further through comments Kant offers on it in the third paragraph of Section 5, Chapter 2 of the Dialectic of the *Critique of Practical Reason*.[25] Here Kant declares that the argument does not show that we have a duty to assume the existence of God. The only duty we have in connection with the moral argument is 'the attempt to produce and further the highest good in the world'. We must in consequence postulate the possibility of the highest good. Significantly, Kant states that '*our reason* finds this thinkable in no other way than on the presupposition of a supreme intelligence' (my emphasis). This hint is expanded upon in the eighth section of Chapter 2, were we are told that the impossibility of conceiving how virtue and happiness can be interconnected in the highest good by means of natural causality is:

> *merely subjective*, i.e. our reason finds it *impossible for it* to conceive, in the mere course of nature, a connection between events, so exactly proportioned and so thoroughly purposive, occurring in the world in accordance with such heterogeneous laws, although, as with every other purposive thing in nature,

it nevertheless cannot prove the impossibility of it in accordance with universal laws of nature, that is show it sufficiently on objective grounds.[26]

What these passages indicate is that the argument operates throughout in the spirit of an exercise in orientation in human thinking. Human agents seek the highest good and need to orient themselves in the right direction for that task. Orientation involves helping themselves to the postulate that there is an intelligent, creator God with the traditional attributes. Such a postulate can provide orientation in pursuit of this end *for beings with intellects like ours*. We have not discovered that nature on its own is not the source of the purposiveness in reality that practical reason requires. We have not discovered that only a God could provide this purposiveness. The upshot of the moral argument is a faith that there is a God which is motivated by reason in its end-seeking guise. This faith is not even on the scale that is flanked by opinion at one end and knowledge at the other.

The elements of the highest good – happiness

The first premise in my summary of Kant's moral argument states that we are under a duty to seek the highest good. The duty is compounded of a duty to become morally perfect and of a rational necessity to seek happiness. Kant unequivocally affirms the necessity of our pursuit of the highest good, telling us that 'Should . . . the highest good be impossible in accordance with practical rules, then the moral law, which commands us to further it, must be fantastic and directed to empty imaginary ends, and must thereby be false in itself'.[27] In particular, if we gave up pursuit of happiness, we would give the pursuit of our specific, material goals. Morality would then be an impossibility, for it provides no specific goals for action by itself. Its role is formal: it yields principles of duty that constrain us in the pursuit of material ends. If we had no material ends, morality would be empty of content.[28]

According to Kant, the necessity we are under to seek happiness is not a moral one. Though I have a duty to promote the well-being of others, I have no direct duty to seek my own happiness. Rather, as condition of rationality in the pursuit of specific non-moral goals, I must seek the overarching goal of happiness. Since he considers that all pursue their own happiness as a matter of natural, rational necessity, then all are unavoidably committed to that end. The problem we face is this: does Kant show that we are under a rational necessity to seek happiness? If he cannot show this, then the first premise of the moral argument fails. Why is Kant so adamant that everyone is under a necessity to seek his or her own happiness? It is surely a plain fact of experience that many people give up the prospect of happiness in the light of other goods they seek, perhaps for large parts of their lives. Many people are placed in circumstances in which they feel they have no choice but to forego the pursuit of personal happiness. Thus people who give up career, leisure pursuits and the like so that they can care for a disabled or sick relative may (if reflective enough) agree that they have given up on happiness. *Contra* Kant, many of them seem able to remain fully committed to fulfilling their obligations even while they give up on happiness. Kant appears to be saying one, or perhaps both, of two things about these individuals: they cannot really be sincere in disavowing the goal of happiness, and/or they would be involved in some kind of irrationality (with their goal of caring clashing with their necessary of goal of happiness). I submit that it is hard to see, independently of our prior commitment to the theory that all must seek their happiness, why these descriptions should be forced upon us.

Perhaps the answer to this line of questioning lies in Kant's account of happiness. But problems now arise, for he defines 'happiness' in three ways: as pleasure, as contentment and as desire satisfaction.[29] The notion of happiness as pleasure is found early on in the second *Critique*. Happiness is there identified with the consciousness that life is accompanied by 'agreeableness'[30] and is linked to an account of the manner in which people, when they act on their desires, seek pleasure and the agreeableness of life, satisfactions that can be measured in terms of duration and magnitude.[31] The contentment notion of happiness comes in when Kant defines happiness as 'satisfaction with one's state'.[32] The happy life as the contented, satisfied life is obviously not to be identified with the life full of agreeable sensations. A life full of such sensations might be found, upon reflection, not to give rise to contentment and satisfaction; it might seem cloying after a short while. A life found satisfying might be like a satisfying day fell walking: something accompanied by pain and struggle. The third account of happiness comes in with this statement, from the second *Critique*: '*Happiness* is the state of a rational being in the world, in whose whole existence *everything goes according his wish and will*'.[33] Happiness is thus getting what you want, fully and completely: the satisfaction of all one's desires. As desire satisfaction, happiness is clearly not the same as having life accompanied by agreeable sensations, since people can, and frequently do, have many desires for things that do not yield agreeable sensations once they are possessed. Not all desires are desires for pleasurable sensations. Not all desires produce agreeable sensations when satisfied, albeit the mere satisfaction of desire may yield a degree of pleasure; nor is desire satisfaction the same thing as living a contented, satisfied life. It depends on what one desires. All of us some of the time have desires which, upon being satisfied, leave us feeling discontented and dissatisfied with life.

There is an important ambiguity in the notion of an 'existence [in which] everything goes according his wish and will'. What I 'wish and will' may refer to my felt desires, what Kant would call my 'inclinations'. Included in my desires in this sense are those for a large glass of whisky every evening. But 'my desires' might also refer to my ends, the things I seek in intentional actions. There is a massive non-overlap between these two classes of 'things I desire' in the lives of all normal people. We seek in action many things for which we have no felt desires (I set out one morning to clean the car) and we choose not to let many felt desires shape the ends we intentionally pursue. I might have a very strong felt desire for a large cream cake, but choose not to act on it because I am in danger of losing my beautiful figure. If we ignore this distinction between notions of desire, we might think we have an easy proof of the theory that all necessarily seek their happiness. It is obviously irrational not to seek maximal satisfaction of one's intentions (that is just a requirement of consistency in rationally planned action). And it is at least initially plausible (though false, as we have seen above) to suppose that happiness consists in satisfying one's felt desires. Mix up these two notions of desire and you might think it obvious that all finite agents are under a rational necessity to seek their happiness.

I conclude that Kant does not show that we are under a rational necessity to seek the overarching goal of happiness. Thus the first premise of his moral argument is indeed in trouble.

The elements of the highest good – virtue

Within the highest good there is the supreme good: virtue or the worthiness to be happy. We act virtuously for Kant (exhibit what he calls a 'good will') when we do what is right because it is right. Our right actions are not merely in accord with the moral law but are motivated by respect for that law. We achieve the supreme good for a human being when we have a constant disposition to act out of respect for the moral law. The fully virtuous individual will always act guided by respect for the moral law.

Virtue is the condition of complete moral strength that the good human being seeks. Its possessor would have the moral strength to resist all motivating factors, such as our desires, that tempt human beings to act contrary to the moral law. This is how Kant defines it in the *Metaphysics of Morals*:

> Virtue is the strength of a human being's maxims in fulfilling his duty. – All strength can be recognized only by the obstacles which it can overcome; in the case of virtue, however, these are natural inclinations, which can come into conflict with the moral purpose, and since it is the human being himself who puts these obstacles in the way of his maxims, virtue is not merely self-constraint (for then one natural inclination could seek to defeat another), but also a constraint in accordance with a principle of inner freedom, therefore through the mere representation of one's duty in accordance with its formal law.[34]

Kant sometimes describes this supreme human good as 'holiness' (*Heiligkeit*), not 'virtue' (*Tugend*). It is a human form of holiness, not like the holiness of God. God's will is automatically in line with the moral law, because he has no finite, physical nature which tempts him to depart from it. So he does not feel the rules of the moral law as restraints. Holiness in God is not therefore moral strength.

Kant's moral argument turns around the fact that if natural causes were the only kind of causes in reality, then there would be no reason to think that by pursuing virtue/holiness we would also be pursuing our happiness. Any crowning of virtue by happiness would be the merest accident and could not be relied on to continue. Only God, as a cause who acts morally, providentially, can make the pursuit of virtue/holiness the means of gaining a consummate happiness. But that is not all. Kant runs a separate argument for the conclusion that we must postulate immortality and God as the only means whereby we can conceive of holiness as possible, let alone the crowning of holiness with happiness.

The argument is in section 4, Chapter 2 of the Dialectic of the *Critique of Practical Reason* (5: 12–24) and can be summarized thus:

1. Holiness is a mode of perfection that no rational being in the sensible world can ever attain at a given point of time.
2. It is nonetheless rationally required.
3. It can only be envisaged via an endless progress towards moral perfection.
4. Such an endless progress requires the thought of immortal life.
5. This still does not enable us to conceive that holiness will ever be attained in our endless duration.
6. So we must suppose that God takes an eternal, timeless perspective on this uninterrupted progress towards moral perfection and counts it as the actual attainment of holiness.
7. He then is able to distribute an appropriate share in the highest good in accordance with his perception of a trajectory towards moral perfection.

Much can be said about this argument. How, for example, can God's point of view on the would-be virtuous individual's endless progress towards moral perfection transform the progress towards into the actual attainment of holiness? And if progress towards perfection would be endless, why do we need an after-life? For at any point in the after-life at which God chooses to treat continuing progress as perfection the individual concerned will still be an infinite way from attaining actual perfection; and that would be true if the progress were judged by what we had done in this three score years and ten.

What is said about virtue/holiness in the argument for the postulate of immortality chimes in with what Kant affirms elsewhere about the unattainability of this supreme good. Thus in the *Metaphysics of Morals* we have 'Virtue is always in *progress* and yet always starts again *from the beginning*. The first point holds because, considered *objectively*, it is an ideal and unattainable, even though it is a duty to approximate constantly to it.'[35] This suggests that the union of virtue and happiness is likewise unattainable, a conclusion also strengthened by delving into Kant's further reflections on happiness. These show that Kant thought that a perfect, sustainable, permanent happiness is impossible for creatures like us. Creatures in time, subject to change, who also have a divided nature, part-moral and part-desirous, can never achieve consummate happiness. Being in time, we are always apt to compare our present state with a possibly better, happier future one. If we did become completely, perfectly satisfied with our lot, we would have achieved a stasis that was quite incompatible with the active, seeking life characteristic of humanity. Moreover, our moral and our sensuous natures are always struggling with each other, as shown in the fact that virtue is a condition of moral *strength* in placing respect for the moral law above inclinations. This divided life militates against consummate happiness for finite creatures in time.[36]

How then can Kant claim that by assuming the existence of God we make intelligible the real possibility of attaining the highest good? It seems that not even God can bring it about. There is a kind of solution to this worry in Kant. It comprises an alternative conception of the highest good. According to this conception, the highest good is not the union of virtue and happiness in the future, everlasting existence of a human being in time. It is rather a state transcending time and the possession of a physical nature, a state in which holiness is gilded with an accompanying blessedness. In this transformed state, brought about by divine grace, the spatio-temporal continuum would have been left behind. We would not have our inclinations satisfied, for we would have left them behind. With them would have gone our conflicted, dual state as both rational and empirical creatures.[37]

Ought implies can

Premise (2) of Kant's moral argument tells us that what we are obliged to attain, it must be possible for us to attain. In the *Critique of Practical Reason* presentation this 'ought implies can' principle is simply taken for granted: 'We should seek to promote the highest good (which must therefore be possible).'[38] Commentators tend to agree that it is self-evident that we cannot have an obligation to bring about x if we it is not possible to actually do so. Put it this way: 'But I cannot Ψ' is a perfect excuse when faced with the demand to Ψ. But matters are not that simple.

First, we note that what we ought to do is 'seek to promote' the highest good. There might be much – minus God's help – that we can do that amounts to *seeking* to advance the highest good. We can pursue virtue in our own lives and in the lives of others. We can build well-ordered communities that exhibit distributive and retributive justice. Living in such communities will aid us all in living the virtuous life and also aid in the spreading of happiness according to desert.

Second, Kant's easy use of the 'ought implies can' principle belies his appeal in other contexts to the usefulness of governing our thought and practice by asymptotic goals. Kant himself recognizes that reason can seek ends that it views at the same time as impossible of attainment. This recognition casts doubt on his 'ought implies can' principle. Concerning the principles which guide reason in the pursuit of completeness in scientific endeavour Kant states:

> they seem to be transcendental, and even though they contain mere ideas for the guidance of the empirical use of reason, which reason can follow only *asymptotically, as it were, i.e. merely approaching, without ever reaching them,* yet they nonetheless possess, as synthetic propositions a priori, objective, but indeterminate validity, and serve as a rule of possible experience, and can even be used, in the treatment of the same, with good success, as heuristic principles.[39]

Why can we not seek the highest good through moral endeavour believing that it cannot be attained, but using the notion of the highest good as a regulative principle and an asymptotic goal? The value of taking the highest good as a necessary goal lies in the fact that there is always something we can do in the light of it that improves the human lot, even while the perfect good for human beings always lies beyond possible attainment. Thus the atheist might view the highest good as having great regulative value, provided that there is always something that can be done that takes us further in moral endeavour.

There is no question that the above treatment of the highest good as a regulative, asymptotic goal will not do for Kant. What seems to be necessary, as he sees it, is some assurance that moral endeavour takes place in a world that is not hostile to it, but is rather cooperating with it. This comes across in his discussion of the psychological, motivational problems faced by the righteous atheist. In the *Critique of Judgement* Kant discusses this individual through the character of Spinoza. What is important for Kant about Spinoza's philosophy is that it denies (at least as Kant sees it) the existence of any teleology in reality. All events are through-and-through determined by laws of causality. While Kant allows that the righteous Spinoza can be aware of particular imperatives of duty and act upon them, such an atheist is faced with the 'falsity' of the moral law. In taking a long-term view of the moral life, atheists would have to concede that it led to utter despair with existence. Such despair would then disable their commitment to morality. This line is suggested by the continuation of Kant's discussion of morality without God in the third *Critique*. At 5:452 he imagines what would happen to 'a righteous man (like Spinoza)' who does his moral duty but has no belief in a reliable connection between the performance of duty and what happens to himself and others. This individual is said to seek unselfishly the good to which the moral law directs his powers. He gets some assistance here and there from external events. But he faces a world that appears to be wholly indifferent to the moral demands driving his conduct:

> Deceit, violence, and envy will always be rife around him, even though he himself is honest, peaceable, and benevolent; and the righteous ones around himself that he meets will, irrespective of their worthiness to be happy, be subject through nature, which takes no account of that, to all the evils of deprivation, diseases, and untimely death like all the other animals on earth, and will always remain thus, until one wide grave engulfs them all (whether honest or dishonest, it counts the same here) and hurls them, who had the ability to believe themselves to be the final end of creation, back into the abyss of the purposeless chaos of matter from which they were taken.

Faced with this bleak vision of a universe without a controlling moral author, the righteous atheist, Kant continues, must assume the existence of God, 'if he is to stay committed to the call of his moral inner destiny and not weaken the respect, through which the moral law immediately influences him to obedience'. Thus: individual moral acts are possible for this atheist, but in the long-term only disabling moral despair awaits.

Options for the atheist

Thus far we have found some serious problems with Kant's non-evidential argument for the postulate of the existence of God. These include: unclarity over the nature of happiness, over whether it is a rationally necessary goal of human striving, and over whether it is attainable even with God's help. To these problems can be added similar unclarity over the nature of moral perfection and its attainability, plus doubts about the 'ought implies can' principle. We have also noted that according to

Kant himself there is a subjective element in getting from the core ideas of the moral argument to acceptance of *God's* existence, that is a supreme creator with attributes like omnipotence, omniscience and omnibenevolence. We have seen that Kant says such a step reflects merely the way 'we' find ourselves thinking about the possible sources of a moral teleology in reality. Critics of Kant may point out in this regard that his 'we' is parochial. In Eastern religions, for example, there may be a firm belief in reality being morally ordered, without a supporting structure of theism. Some kind of impersonal reality (such as *karma*) might be pictured as the source of moral order.

The last point indicates that there are problems with Kant's fourth step:

4. Moral order and moral causality can only be conceived to be possible if we postulate a God as their moral source.

These problems can be exploited by atheistic critics of the argument. In doing so, they can build upon further concessions made by Kant. The possibility posed by his own writings is that forms of atheism are untouched by his moral argument.

To see how forms of atheism could survive Kant's argument we should consider how he characterises atheism. In the *Lectures on Rational Theology* Kant distinguishes dogmatic atheism from sceptical atheism and declares that it is to the former type of atheism that moral theism stands opposed.[40] Dogmatic atheists cannot practise morality. They must be the most evil of human beings if they are genuine in their atheism. They are dogmatic in 'directly' denying the existence of God and in declaring it impossible that there is God at all. Sceptical atheists, in contrast, find no proof that there is a God but acknowledge that there is a real possibility that God exists. Kant offers a significant comment on this kind of atheism: 'Now indeed the belief in a merely possible God as world ruler is obviously the minimum of theology; but is of great enough influence, that for a human being, who already recognizes the necessity of his duties with apodeictic certainty, it can call forth his morality'.[41] There are other places where Kant states that acknowledgement of the mere possibility that there might be a God will provide the minimum of theology that morality needs to work.[42] As long as someone takes 'There is a God' to be possibly true, he or she can use it as a working hypothesis in guiding the pursuit of ends.

So Kant's remarks on the force of the moral argument point in two ways. In the main, he contends that the argument is productive of faith in God, where this is a firm holding-as-true based on non-evidential grounds. In some places, he appears to imply that all that respect for the goal of the highest good needs is entertaining the possibility of God's existence.

It may be objected on Kant's behalf at this point that he has grounds for demanding more from the atheist than 'it is possible, in some way or other, that the highest good is attainable'. To give substance to the underlying 'ought implies can' principle, we need to be assured that highest good is really possible, and not merely notionally possible. How can we be assured that there is a real possibility that we are members of a teleological order unless we believe in some ground for that possibility? Such assurance entails we must have a positive faith in some ground of teleology. God as the ground of moral teleology makes that teleology really possible.

This defence of Kant is undermined by two crucial points of Kant's own making. In the first place, Kant's Critical teaching on what must be added to formal consistency to make something really possible is not God, but experience. It is the totality of things in the empirical world that grounds real possibility.[43] In his Critical phase he consistently rejects the notion that appeal to super sensible realities can give us insight into the grounds of real possibility. In addition, we have already quoted the significant passage from the *Critique of Practical Reason* (5: 145), where in glossing the force of the moral argument, Kant states that the ground of the moral argument is *merely subjective*, depending on what our reason finds it *impossible for it* to conceive. So: the argument as presented rules out appeal to God as illuminating the real possibility of the highest good.

There is thus a real question of whether atheists must abandon the belief that the highest good is possible of attainment if the moral argument is sound. Sceptical atheists, admitting the possibility that there is God, definitely need not abandon the possibility of the highest good. They acknowledge the possibility of a God whose existence would entail that the highest good would come about, and thus they can acknowledge the possibility of the highest good. Dogmatic atheists might appear to be in a hopeless position with regard to the possibility of the highest good. However, Kant's concession at 5:145 that reason 'nevertheless cannot prove the impossibility of it [the agreement of morality and nature] in accordance with universal laws of nature, that is show it sufficiently on objective grounds' might give dogmatic atheists some room for manoeuvre. Why can they not say that, though they are convinced that is not possible that the God of theism exists, the fact of the authority of the drive to the highest good indicates that there must be *some* non-theistic way in which moral worth is connected to happiness in the long run?

There appear to be two distinct issues here. One is whether such a moral teleology can *only* be thought of as obtaining through the effect of an intelligence, that is a reality that conceives of goals and is aware of such things as someone's moral worth. The second issue concerns whether such an intelligence need be thought of as a transcendent creator. On the first issue, we have noted that in Eastern thought the concept of *karma* is precisely that of a moral mechanism in reality that, in at least some systems, operates independently of gods or a God. On the second issue, we can note that pantheistic systems such as Stoicism have a central place for an intelligent principle that rules the world of nature while yet conceiving of that intelligence as immanent and embodied in nature. Why can there not be room then for dogmatic atheists to rule out theism while leaving the highest good's possibility to be grounded on some unknown moral mechanism? Kant's easy assumption in central places in his corpus[44] that only theism will ground belief in the highest good seems contrary to the spirit of the Critical Philosophy. The concession from the *Critique of Practical Reason* 5:145 quoted above appears, in contrast, to be much more in keeping with a philosophy that tells us we cannot know things as they are in themselves. We can ask what is wrong with the stance of someone who, reading 5:145, simply states: 'it is incumbent on me to pursue the highest good; this end must therefore be realisable; but I do not know enough to speculate on how it might be realizable; it must be realizable some way or other'.[45] This criticism of Kant can accept that rational agents need to orient themselves in relation to the moral life. It can accept that part of the orientation consists in setting the highest good as a goal of moral striving. All it then needs is the assumption that there is some mechanism, either immanent or transcendent, whereby the highest good will come about through such striving.

Conclusion

I have used a contemporary argument from Robert Adams to illustrate evidential moral arguments for God's existence and a justly famous piece of reasoning in Kant to illustrate the non-evidential forms. Discussion of both suggests this conclusion. Someone who is, on other grounds, inclined to regard the supposition of an all-perfect creator as intellectually flawed is not going to meet in moral arguments for God something that has to change their mind, on pain of irrationality. Moral arguments of both types involve consideration of wide-ranging issues concerning the nature of moral judgements and the ends of the moral life. The issues connected with these two facets of morality are highly ramified and controversial. This means that one disposed not to believe or accept that there is God has plenty of room to deny key premises of these arguments and/or question important inferences in them.

Notes

1 In this chapter references to Kant's writings will be to volume and page number of the Academy Edition of his *Gesammelte Shriften* (in the case of the *Critique of Pure Reason* to page numbers of the first edition (A) and the second edition (B)). Translations are my own.

Dates are given below for works published in Kant's lifetime.
Critique of Judgement [*Kritik der Urtheilskraft*, 1790, G.S. Vols 20 and 5].
Critique of Pure Reason [Kritik der reinen Vernunft, 1781/1787, G.S. Vols 4/3].
Critique of Practical Reason [*Kritik der praktischen Vernunft*, 1788, G.S. Vol. 5].
Groundwork of the Metaphysics of Morals [*Grundlegung zur Metaphysik der Sitten*, 1785, G.S. Vol. 4].
Lectures on Ethics [*Vorlesungen über Moralphilosophie*, G.S. Vol. 27].
Lectures on Rational Theology [Vorlesungen über Rationaltheologie, G.S. Vol. 28].
Metaphysics of Morals [Die Metaphysik der Sitten, 1797, G.S. Vol. 6].
Moral Mongrovius II [*G.S* Vol. 29].
Reflexionen [*G.S.* Vols 17, 18, and 19].
Religion within the Boundaries of Bare Reason [Die Religion innerhalb der Grenzen der bloßen Vernunft, 1793/1794, G.S. Vol. 6].
What Real Progress Has Metaphysics Made in Germany since the Time of Leibniz and Wolff?

[Welches sind die wirklichen Fortschritte, die die Metaphysik seit Leibnizens und Wolff's Zeiten in Deutschland gemacht hat?, G.S. Vol. 20].

2   The important distinction between belief and acceptance will be explained later in this chapter.
3   See Oppy, G. *Arguing about Gods*. (Cambridge: Cambridge University Press, 2006), 4–5.
4   *Critique of Pure Reason*, Bxxx.
5   *Critique of Practical Reason*, 5:126. For an account of 'faith' in Kant see Byrne, P. A. *Kant on God*. (Aldershot: Ashgate, 2007), 77–82.
6   Meta-ethics is that branch of philosophy that considers the logical and epistemic status of moral judgements.
7   See Kant *Groundwork of the Metaphysics of Morals*, 4:414.
8   Adams, R. 'Moral Arguments for the Existence of God', R. Adams *The Virtue of Faith*. (New York: Oxford University Press, 1987), 144–63.
9   *Op. cit.*, 145.
10 For a survey of such meta-ethical theories see Geoff Sayre-McCord 'Metaethics', *Stanford Encyclopedia of Philosophy*. http://plato.stanford.edu/entries/metaethics/, and follow the links to related articles.
11 *Cf.* Shaw, J. 'Divine commands at the foundations of morality'. *Canadian Journal of Philosophy* (2002), 32, 424–26.
12 For a lengthy defence and exposition of this view see Shafer-Landau, R. *Moral Realism*. (New York: Oxford University Press, 2003.)
13 Hume, D. *A Treatise of Human Nature*, L. A. Selby-Bigge (ed.). (Oxford: Clarendon Press, 1975), 457.
14 *Critique of Practical Reason*, 5:25.
15 See Allison, H. E. *Kant's Theory of Freedom*. (Cambridge: Cambridge University Press, 1990), 68.
16 See *Metaphysics of Morals*, 6:227, *Lectures on Ethics*, 27:283 and *Moral Mongrovious II*, 29, 633–34.
17 *Groundwork of the Metaphysics of Morals* 4:14.
18 *Critique of Practical Reason*, 5:113–32.
19 *Critique of Practical Reason*, 5:125.
20 *Critique of Practical Reason*, 5:146.
21 See *Critique of Pure Reason* A822/B850–A823/B851.
22 For a full account of the relation between belief and acceptance see Alston, W. P. 'Audi on non-doxastic faith', in M. Timmons, J. Green and A. Mele (eds), *Rationality and the Good: Critical Essays on the Ethics and Epistemology of Robert Audi*. (New York: Oxford University Press, 2007), 123–39.
23 *Critique of Pure Reason*, A829/B857.
24 *Critique of Judgement*, 5:450$_n$.
25 *Critique of Practical Reason*, 125–6.
26 *Critique of Practical Reason*, 5:145.

27 *Critique of Practical Reason*, 5:114.

28 See Mariña, J. 'Making sense of Kant's highest good'. *Kant-Studien* (2000), 91, 344.

29 See Wood, A. W. 'Kant versus eudaimonism', in P. Cicovacki (ed.), *Kant's Legacy: Essays in Honour of Lewis White Beck.* (Rochester: University of Rochester Press, 2001), 266; A much more detailed survey of Kant's various notions of happiness can be found in Wike, V. S. *Kant on Happiness in Ethics.* (Albany: State University of New York Press, 1994).

30 *Critique of Practical Reason*, 5:22.

31 *Critique of Practical Reason*, 5:23.

32 *Metaphysics of Morals*, 6:387.

33 *Critique of Practical Reason*, 5:124.

34 *Metaphysics of Morals*, 6:394.

35 *Metaphysics of Morals*, 6:409.

36 For an exposition of these points see Byrne *op. cit.*, 107–9.

37 This conception of the highest good is documented in Mariña, J., *op. cit.*

38 *Critique of Practical Reason*, 5:125.

39 *Critique of Pure Reason*, A663/B691; my emphasis.

40 *Lectures on Rational Theology*, 28:1010.

41 *Lectures on Rational Theology*, 28:1010.

42 See *What Real Progress Has Metaphysics Made in Germany since the Time of Leibniz and Wolff?* 20:305, *Reflexionen* 18:315, *Religion within the Boundaries of Bare Reason*, 6:153n.

43 See *Critique of Pure Reason*, A581–82/B608–9.

44 See, for example, *Critique of Judgement*, 5:540–41.

45 See Denis, L. 'Kant's criticisms of atheism'. *Kant-Studien* (2003), 94, 216.

CHAPTER 7

WILLIAM JAMES AND RELIGIOUS EXPERIENCE

Richard M. Gale

No one did more to promote the cause of religious experience than William James (1842–1910). He accomplished this in his great 1902 masterpiece, *The Varieties of Religious Experience*,[1] wherein he passionately and persuasively argued for these two theses. The first holds that the basis of religion, including its theology, institutional structure and beliefs, is rooted in religious experiences of a mystical sort in which the individual has an apparent direct, nonsensory perception of a 'More', an 'Unseen' supernatural or purely spiritual reality into which she is to some extent absorbed and from which spiritual energy flows into her. The second thesis, which alone is the concern of this paper, is that these religious experiences are cognitive in the sense of being revelatory of or evidence for objective aspects of reality. Defences of the cognitivity of religious experiences of the mystical sort have become a growth industry in recent years, and William James has been one of the main inspirations for this. James's defence of cognitivity is important not only in its own right but also as providing background that can help us gain a deeper understanding of these contemporary defences, thereby giving us an extra incentive to pay a return visit to William James.

James gives pride of place among religious experiences to mystical experiences, both of the monistic sort favoured by Eastern mystics in which there is an identity between the subject and object of the experience and the dualistic ones that are prominent within the Western theistic traditions that recognize a numerical distinction between God and the experiencer. His reason for doing so is that he sees them as the most extreme and intense forms of religious experience, and his methodological rule is to consider a given phenomenon in its most extreme and developed form. Even if this methodological rule is not acceptable, James is justified in giving pride of place to mystical experiences because historically they have been accorded the greatest significance, no doubt because among all the varieties of religious experience, they have the strongest claim for being cognitive since they seem to give us the same sort of evidence for the existence of their apparent object as ordinary sense experiences do for their apparent object.

Before James attempts to establish the cognitivity of mystical experiences he attempts to elucidate their nature by giving numerous quotations from both monistic and dualistic mystics, from which he then attempts to extract the salient features of mystical experiences. One of them is that mystics take their experiences to be perceptual, likening them to ordinary sense perceptions in that both involve a direct acquaintance with an object, although only the latter has a sensory content. 'Mystical experiences are . . . direct perceptions . . . absolutely sensational . . . face to face presentation of what seems to exist' (336). A perception is 'direct', I assume, if the existential claims made by the subject on the basis of her experience are noninferential. James claims that mystical experiences, like sensory ones, are intentional in the sense that they have an apparent accusative that exists independently of the subject when the experience is veridical. In this respect, they are unlike a feeling of pain, which takes only a cognate or internal accusative, since feeling a pain is nothing but paining or feeling painfully. It will be seen that the proposition that mystical experiences are perceptual is employed in James's argument for their cognitivity based on their being analogous to ordinary sensory perceptions. Therefore, if this proposition is false, as well it might be, his analogical argument collapses.

James tries to take a neutral stance on whether mystical experiences support a monistic or pluralistic view of the More or Unseen reality, in spite of his own strong emotional commitment to the pluralistic version. At one place he seems to come down on the side of the modern-day mystical ecumenicalists, Suzuki, Stace and Merton, who contend that there is a common phenomenological *monistic* core to all unitive mystical experiences that then gets interpreted by mystics so as to accord with the underlying culture of their society. 'In mystic states we both become one with the Absolute and we become aware of our oneness. *This is the everlasting and triumphant mystical tradition, hardly altered by differences of clime or creed'* (332, my italics). Some of James's major contentions in *The Varieties of Religious Experience*, however, require a dualistic experience. For example, James says that prayer is 'the very soul and essence of religion', and then describes prayer as involving two-way interaction between two subjects. James's strong Protestant leanings cause him, for the most part, to give a dualistic interpretation of mystical experiences as Western theistic mystics have done.

One of the features of mystical experiences, as well as conversion experiences in general, that James stresses, so much so that it is used as one of the four defining conditions of a mystical experience, is that the subject is passive in respect to them. While persons can take steps, such as following the mystical way, to help induce the experience, its coming is viewed by religious mystics as the free bestowal of a gift upon them by the grace of God. Through the experience the subject feels that her conscious will is held in abeyance as she finds absorption in a higher unity. 'The mystic feels as if his own will were grasped and held by a superior power' (303). In both cases there must be a cancelling out of the finite so as to open ourselves to the infinite. This resignation and abandonment of the finite self and its conscious will is found in the mystical and conversion experience of both James's once- and twice-born, and healthy- and morbid-minded persons.

James, no doubt with his sick soul's experiences of existential angst in mind, stresses how such mystically-based resignation cannot 'fail to steady the nerves, to cool the fever, and appease the fret, if one be conscious that, no matter what one's difficulties for the moment may appear to be, one's life as a whole is in the keeping of a power whom one can absolutely trust' (230). The mystical experiences that such submission of the conscious will helps to foster are 'reconciling and unifying states' that 'tell of the supremacy of the ideal, of vastness, of union, of safety, and of rest' (330 and 339). In such mystical union there is a 'life not correlated with death, a health not liable to illness, a kind of good that will not perish, a good in fact that flies beyond the Goods of nature' (119).

A theme that runs throughout *The Varieties of Religious Experience* is the insufficiency of meliorism – that good will win out over evil in the long run if we collectively exert our best moral effort – because it cannot give us this sort of assurance that, in spite of all the known evils of the world, all is well. It is condemned as being 'the very consecration of forgetfulness and superficiality' (118–9). But in his *Pragmatism* he ardently defends a version of meliorism. He tingles with excitement at the thought that we are engaged in a Texas death match with evil, without any assurance that we shall succeed. A James interpreter faces a daunting challenge to reconcile James's mysticism with his pragmatism.

There are other apparent clashes between his mysticism and pragmatism. First there is the clash between his pragmatism's activistic or promethean self and the passive self of the mystic. The promethean self *is* the active will, which, James says, is 'the substantive thing which we are'.[2] But for the mystic the true self, that 'self of all the other selves', no longer is identified with the active aspect of a person, their free conscious will. Quite the contrary, it is that very self, along with its promethean will to believe and the meliorism it favours, that must be surrendered. The true or higher self is that aspect of us, identified by James with the subconscious or transmarginal self, that is able to enter into a complete or partial union with a supersensible reality, which is a 'More' of the same kind as it.

The mystical self displaces the active will by 'a willingness to close our mouths and be as nothing in the floods and waterspouts of God' (46). 'To give up one's conceit of being good, is the only door to the Universe's deeper reaches'.[3] By meeting despair with religious resignation, we uncover 'resources in us that naturalism, with its literal virtue, never recks of, possibilities that take our breath away, and show a world wider than either physics or Philistine ethics can imagine. Here is a world in which all is well, *in spite* of certain forms of death, indeed *because* of certain forms of death, death of hope, death of strength, death of responsibility, of fear and worry'.[4] The death of strength and responsibility is the death of the promethean moral agent, along with its melioristic religion. 'Sincerely to give up one's conceit or hope of being good in one's own right is the only door to the universe's deeper reaches'.[5] The overcoming of our active self does not assure that we will achieve some kind of experiential union with God, but it is a necessary first-step along the way to such mystical illumination.

Yet another tension between James's pragmatism and mysticism concerns the nature of reality- or existential-claims. According to his pragmatism which world qualifies as the actual world is relative to the passing interests of an agent.[6] Thus, all such claims must be qualified by restriction to a particular perspective of some agent at a given time, as, for example, *qua* scientist, I say that there is thorough going causal determinism but *qua* moral agent I say we possess a free will that is not determined by prior causes.

Mysticism also challenges James's pragmatic theory of meaning and truth. The pragmatic theory of meaning holds that the meaning of X is a set of propositions predicting what experience will be had upon performing certain operations. In this connection think of how a chemist would define a substance, such as gold, in terms of the experiments by which it is determined that something is gold – if you place it in aqua regia, you shall see it dissolve. A belief in the reality of X becomes true when these predictions are verified. But the mystic's conception of the Absolute, the undifferentiated unity, the eternal one, God is not based on how we can ride herd on it, for there is nothing that we do to or with this mystical reality, or ways in which it is expected to behave if we perform certain operations. It doesn't dissolve in aqua regia. It simply *is*, and is just what it *appears* to be in the immediate experience of the mystic. A door to door salesman of mystical reality, therefore, would be stymied when asked, 'But what does it do?' or 'What can I do with it?' Herein the content of the proposition that this reality exists is not reducible to any set of pragmatic conditionalized predictions. The star performer finally gets into the act, unlike the case of the pragmatically favoured melioristic religion, which reduced 'God exists' to the conditionalized prediction that good will win out over evil in the long run, if we collectively exert our best moral effort. The reason James chose meliorism as his example of a religion in the final lecture of *Pragmatism* is that it can be shown to employ the same pragmatic theory of meaning and truth as does science, which fits his program of reconciliation between science and religion through methodological univocalism.

In order to account for the meaning of mystical reality-claims James will have to resort to a nonpragmatic content empiricism. Since the meaningful content of the mystic's reality-claim is based on the manner in which she is phenomenologically appeared to in an of-God type experience, the truth of the claim will depend on whether her experience is objective or cognitive. The spiritual and moral benefits that the experience occasions, as will be seen, become relevant, but only as a means of indirect verification, there now being, as there wasn't for meliorism, a distinction between direct and indirect verification, with an assertion's meaning being identified primarily with the former, that being the apparent object of the mystical experience. James seems to recognize this when he says that 'the word 'truth' is here taken to mean something additional to bare value for life' (401). Accordingly, James makes the issue of the cognitivity or objectivity of mystical experience a central issue in *The Varieties of Religious Experience*. Concerning them, he asks about their 'metaphysical significance' (308), 'cognitivity' (324), 'authoritativeness' (335), 'objective truth' (304), 'value for knowledge' (327), their 'truth' (329) and whether they 'furnish any *warrant for the truth* of the . . . supernaturality and pantheism which they favor' (335), or are 'to be taken as *evidence* . . . for the actual existence of a higher world with which our world is in relation' (384). James is quite explicit that the answer to the 'objectivity' question is independent of the biological and psychological benefits that accrue from mystical experiences.

James concludes that there is a generic content of the many different type of mystical experiences that 'is literally and objectively true' (405). His arguments for this are not made sufficiently explicit, but with a little sympathetic imagination and anachronistic hindsight I believe that two arguments can be detected in the text: the argument from analogy with sense experience and the argument from an inference to the best explanation. The former is far more important and will be considered first.

This argument has been very ably defended in recent years by William Wainwright, Richard Swinburne, Gary Gutting, Keith Yandell, Jerome Gellman and especially William Alston, whose book, *Perceiving God*, should become a classic.[7] First, an overview will be given of a generic brand version of their arguments, and then an attempt shall be made to locate it, or at least the germ of it, in James, hopefully without being anachronistic to the point of developing a private history of philosophy. It is an argument from analogy that goes as follows. Mystical and sense experiences are analogous in cognitively relevant respects; and, since the latter are granted to be cognitive, so should the former, in which a cognitive type of experience is one that counts, in virtue of some *a priori* presumptive inference rule, as evidence or warrant for believing that the apparent object of the experience, its intentional accusative, objectively exists and is as it appears to be in the experience. For sense experience the presumptive inference rule is that if it perceptually appears to be the case that X exists, then probably it is the case that X exists, unless there are defeating conditions. These defeating conditions consist in tests and checks for the veridicality of the experience that get flunked on this occasion. Prominent among these tests are agreement among relevant observers, law-like coherence between the experience's content and the content of earlier and later experiences, and being caused in the right way. The presumptive inference rule is said to be *a priori*, because it cannot be justified by appeal to sense experience without vicious epistemic circularity because the justification makes use of propositions that require the truth of the conclusion. Think of the sort of vicious epistemic circularity in attempts to justify inductive reasoning by an argument that employs inductive reasoning – inductive reasoning has usually worked in the past – or to justify reliance on apparent memories by an argument that makes use of propositions that rest on apparent memories.

If mystical experiences are to be subject to an analogous *a priori* presumptive inference rule, they must be analogous to sense experiences in having defeating conditions – checks and tests that can get flunked. All of the contemporary defenders of the cognitivity of mystical experiences argue that the great religious mystical traditions employ a fairly elaborate network of tests for veridicality of mystical experiences, usually including that the subject, as well as her community, display favourable moral and/or spiritual development as a result of the experience, that what her experience reveals accords with her religion's holy scriptures and the mystical experiences of past saints and notables, to name some of the more important tests of most of the great religious mystical traditions.

These tests are admittedly not exactly analogous to those that inform the sense experience doxastic practice in that, most notably, they do not contain any requirements for being caused-in-the-right-way requirement or having nomic connections between the content of the experience and those of earlier and later experiences.[8] An attempt is made to explain away these disanalogies by showing that they can be accounted for in terms of a categorical difference between the intentional accusatives of the two types of experience, those being material objects for sense experiences and God (the eternal one, etc.) for mystical experiences. Whereas material objects, for the most part, behave according to scientific laws, and thus permit predictions to be made of future experiences and a distinction to be drawn between a right and a wrong way for a sense experience to be caused, God, being an absolutely free supernatural being, precludes our being able to predict how he will behave and, in particular, when and to whom he will choose to directly to reveal himself, as well as our being able to distinguish between a right and a wrong way for an of-God type of experience to occur. Given that God supernaturally causes a mystical experience by his efficacious will, there is no causal chain of events linking God with a mystical experience in the way in which there is such a chain linking a material object with a veridical perception of it.

With a little imagination we can find most, but not all, of the elements of this analogical argument in *The Varieties of Religious Experience*; in fact, a good case can be made out that James deserves to be credited with being the founding father of this argument. In the first place, James makes a prominent use of a perceptual model of mystical experience, which is the analogical premise of the contemporary argument for cognitivity. He comes right out and says:

> Our own more 'rational' beliefs are based on evidence exactly similar in nature to that which mystics quote for theirs. Our senses, namely, have assured us of certain states of fact; but mystical experiences are as direct perceptions of fact for those who have them as any sensations ever were for us. The records show that even though the five senses be in abeyance in them, they are absolutely sensational in their epistemological quality. (336)

Furthermore, like the contemporary analogical arguers, James goes on to fill out the analogy by showing that there are mystical analogues for some of the tests for the veridicality of sense experience. What is apparently revealed by mystical experiences 'must be sifted and tested, and run the gauntlet of confrontation with the total context of experience just like what comes from the outer world of sense' (338). Mystical experiences are also likened to 'windows through which the mind looks out upon a more extensive and inclusive world' than is revealed by our senses, and just as we have checks and tests for mediating between rival sensory-based claims there are analogous ones for mediating between rival mystically-based claims. Because of these background defeating conditions, it will be possible for mysticism to have 'its valid experiences and its counterfeit ones, just as our world has them . . . We should have to use its experiences by selecting and subordinating and substituting just as is our custom in this ordinary naturalistic world; we should be liable to error just as we are now' (339). Further indication of just how close James is to the contemporary analogical arguers is his claim that mystical experiences 'establish a presumption' in favour of the thing being as it appears to be in them (336), which sounds very much like their presumptive inference rule.

If James did accept such a presumptive inference rule, he would not be committing the howler of inferring that the apparent object of a mystical experience objectively exists from the mere fact that it appears to exist to its subject, as he seems to do in the following: 'The theologian's contention that the religious man is moved by an external power is vindicated, for one of the peculiarities of invasions from the subconscious region is that they take on objective appearances, and suggest to the Subject an external control' (403). James seemingly drops the intentional operator 'take on' and 'suggest' as he moves from the 'seeming'-premise to the 'objectively is' conclusion. Given the presumptive inference rule, the inference becomes valid provided the conclusion is weakened to, 'It probably is the case that the apparent object of a mystical experience exists'. In other words, a mystical experience, like a sensory one, bestows only a prima facie warrant to believe that the apparent object exists. The belief is defeasible because of the battery of background overriders or defeaters that can be flunked.

There is one very important respect in which James differs from contemporary analogical arguers that renders his argument less attractive than theirs, namely he completely eschews any attempt to place the relevant background tests, which are the overriders or defeaters, within the shared practices of an ongoing religious community. In general, James's failure to see the importance of religious institutions, with their shared beliefs and communal practices, is a significant limitation in the account that is given of religious experience in The Varieties of Religious Experience. James over glorifies the isolated individual. His mystic is a lone gun mystic, cut off from any doxastic practice of an ongoing religious community. From where his mystic gets her tests from and how they are enforced remains a mystery. Just as James was committed to a private language in which the speaker follows rules that only she can determine are being followed correctly, James's mystic, in virtue of being isolated from a community of fellow believers and practitioners, must follow her own private tests.

Contemporary analogical arguers are intent on justifying the various ongoing mystical doxastic practices as being reliable for the most part. James, on the other hand, works only on the *retail* level, his concern being exclusively with the justification for an individual mystic taking one of her experiences to be veridical. He fails to see that this justification cannot be cut off from the *wholesale* justification of the shared social practice of basing objective existential claims on mystical experiences. James fails to realize that by eschewing the wholesale level, he significantly weakens the effectiveness of his will to believe justification for the lone mystic believing that one of her experiences is veridical, in which a will to believe justification is based on the desirable consequences of believing a proposition for which there is no adequate evidence. This is a very important application of the will to believe, since what she believes in this matter could have the most important consequences for her future moral and spiritual development, that is, for her quest for sanctification. Certainly, she will be aided in her attempt to get herself to believe on will to believe grounds that her mystical experience is veridical if she first believes that the general doxastic practice of basing existential claims on mystical experiences is a reliable one that yields true existential beliefs for the most part. This belief also must be based on will to believe grounds, since the mystical doxastic practice, like the sensory one, does not admit of any noncircular external justification. James's analogical argument, along with his will to believe justification for believing in the veridicality of an individual mystical experience, welcome supplementation by bringing in the doxastic practice in which his tests are embedded.

With this in mind, a survey can now be made of the different tests he recognized as relevant to determining the veridicality of a mystical experience. Like the contemporary analogical arguers, James recognizes a mystical analogue to the sensory agreement and prediction tests, though he adds a third one – the immediate luminosity test. Here, in brief, is how they work.

James makes a very broad application of the agreement test so that it concerns not only whether there is agreement among the mystics themselves but whether their reports agree with ordinary sensory-based ones. In regard to the former, he first says that there is a consensus among mystics and that 'it would be odd . . . if such a unanimous type of experience should prove to be altogether wrong' (336). However, he immediately counters that 'the appeal to numbers has no logical force' and that there is considerable disagreement among the monistic and pluralistic mystics, not to mention their collective disagreement with demoniacal mysticism. Not only doesn't the agreement test support the objectivity of mystical experience when only mystical experiences are considered, it counts against this when the sensory-based experiences are brought in. Mystical experiences 'do not come to everyone; and the rest of life makes either no connexion with them, or tends to contradict them more than it confirms them' (336). And, against the claims of monistic mystics, James says that the 'eaches' of the pluralists 'are at any rate real enough to have made themselves at least appear to everyone, whereas the absolute has as yet appeared immediately to only a few mystics, and indeed to them very ambiguously'.[9]

James, I believe, tries to soften this clash between mysticism and sense experience by giving a very understated conclusion concerning what mystical experiences ultimately proclaim.

> As a rule, mystical states merely add a supersenuous meaning to the ordinary outward data of consciousness. They are excitements like the emotions of love or ambition, flights to our spirit by means of which facts already objectively before us fall into a new life. They do not contradict these facts as such, or deny anything that our senses have immediately seized. (338)

The same protective strategy seems operative in James's bizarre initial set of four defining characteristics of a mystical experience – being ineffable, noetic, transitory and passive (302–3) – in which he fails to include being a unitive experience, which is their most important and distinctive feature, but one that seems to clash with the deliverances of ordinary sense experience, which presents us with a multiplicity of distinct objects in space and time.[10] This aptly could be called the 'comic book' theory of mystical experiences, since they are supposed to function as do the field of force lines that comic books place around an object that is perceived or thought in a specially intense manner. This, at best, fits the experiences at the undeveloped end of the mystical spectrum, such as drunkenness, but not those unitive experiences at the developed end, which not only report new facts, James's higher dimensions of reality, but also sometimes seem to contradict our sensory-based beliefs concerning the reality of space, time and multiplicity. James does not want us to have to serve on a jury and decide whether to believe the testimony of the mystics or that of the vast majority of mankind, but he does not map out any effective strategy for preventing the matter from going to trial. He wants to find some common denominator of all mystical experiences that is sufficiently watered down so as not to conflict with the deliverances of sense experience, but this fails to address the issue of whether the more developed mystical experiences are veridical.

Whereas, according to James, the agreement test did not offer any support to the objectivity claim of mystics, even counting against it, the prediction test does. Because of the passive and transitory nature of mystical experiences, we are not able to predict their occurrence, and, to this extent, the prediction test counts against their objectivity. But this is more than offset by the fact that so many mystics grow morally and/or spiritually as a result of their experience. In attacking reductivistic causal explanations of mystical experiences he says that we must 'inquire into their fruits for life', rather than their causes (327). This is an ongoing theme in *The Varieties of Religious Experience*, especially in Lectures I, XIV and XV.

Unfortunately, James does not clearly distinguish between these good consequences being epistemologically confirmatory of the *proposition* believed and their pragmatically justifying in the will to believe manner our *believing* it. The following is a typical example of this unclarity. 'Believing that a higher power will take care of us in certain ways better than we can take care of ourselves, if we only genuinely throw ourselves upon it and consent to use it, it finds the belief, not only not impugned, but corroborated by it observation [of good consequences]' (103 my italics) Belief is being used here in a way that is ambiguous between the psychological state or act of believing and the what-is-believed, the proposition. This opens James to the standard objection that he ran together the psychological benefits of believing a proposition with the confirmation of the proposition believed. It is here that James is far outstripped by his contemporary analogical arguers, such as Alston, who makes clear in his use of the prediction test that the good consequence for the mystic and her community are confirmatory of the objectivity of the mystical experience in virtue of a conceptual or categorical link between these consequences and the nature of the apparent object of the experience. Since God is essentially good, it is probable that those who have had an objective experience of him will benefit morally and spiritually. By the same reasoning, one should count the deleterious consequence of a mystical experience as evidence for it having been a veridical perception of a malevolent being like the devil.

Immediate luminosity, the subject's intense feeling of delight and reality, figures prominently in James's network of confirmatory tests, sometimes being accorded pride of place over good consequence (23) and at others taking second place to them (21–2). An interesting question is why James, unlike his contemporary analogical arguers, used this test. The answer might be that his pragmatic-interest-relative account of existence, although not explicitly endorsed in *The Varieties of Religious Experience*, still weighs heavily in James's thinking. This might account for James's seeming relativization of *being evidence for* to persons in his first two conclusions regarding what mystical experiences establish.

1. Mystical states, when well developed, usually are, and have the right to be, absolutely authoritative over the individuals to whom they come.
2. No authority emanates from them which should make it a duty for those who stand outside of them to accept their revelations uncritically (335).

This makes it look as if the occurrence of mystical states constitutes evidence for their objectivity for those who have them but not for those who do not, which clearly violates the principle of universalizability of *being evidence for* among persons, as well as times. If *E* is evidence for proposition *p*, then *E* is evidence for any person (or at any time) that *p* is true. *Being evidence for* is an existentially grounded relation and must not be confused with *being taken to be evidence for*, which is relative to a person's epistemic situation – what she knows and believes. The appearance of certain symptoms could be taken as evidence for cholera by a physician but not a lay person. What mystics know that many nonmystics do not, is that mystical experiences occur and therefore that there exists certain evidence for the existence of God. Non-mystics can have only indirect knowledge through the testimony of mystics that such evidence obtains; and, as a consequence, they have less epistemic warrant for believing that mystical states occur than do the mystics themselves. But given the great number of reports of mystical experiences and the obvious sincerity and competence of those making such a claim, very little probability is lost between the report of mystics to have had a mystical experience and a non-mystic's claim that such experiences occur.

How might James defend himself against the charge that he confounded *being evidence for* with *being taken to be evidence for*? One way is to appeal to his doctrine that truth is relative to persons. There are a few passages, but only a few, in *Pragmatism* and *The Meaning of Truth* where he seems to say that merely personal, psychological satisfaction counts a confirmatory of a belief's truth. Two persons believing the same proposition might have different personal satisfactions that accrue from their belief and thus the proposition might be true for one of them but not the other. James's appeal to immediate luminosity as a prominent test for the veridicality of a mystical experience seems to be a case in point, since such a feeling can vary across persons, the non-mystic not sharing the mystic's feeling of immediate luminosity. This defence has a very limited appeal, since most critics of James, in particular John Dewey, have berated him for occasionally confounding consequences of a belief that are confirmatory of the proposition believed and those, such as psychological satisfaction, that justify in a will to believe manner holding the belief.

Maybe the best that James can do is to say that the mystic has a will to believe justification for taking her experience to be veridical that a non-mystic does not, since having this belief will have beneficial consequences for her that the non-mystic's belief in its veridicality will not have. The mystic's belief in the veridicality of her experience will be an aid in her quest for sanctification but the non-mystic's belief in the experience's veridicality will not aid the non-mystic in her own quest for sanctification.

James's second argument for the cognitivity of mystical experience, based on an inference to the best explanation, is only hinted at in *The Varieties of Religious Experience* on pages 303, 304 and 381, being more fully developed in other works. Mystical states, like many other psychic or paranormal phenomena, among which James recognized telepathy and alternative or secondary personality, such as prophetic speech, automatic writing, hypnotic and mediumistic trances, all admit of explanation if we follow Frederic Myers and Gustav Fechner and posit 'a continuum of cosmic consciousness, against which individuality builds accidental fences, and into which our several minds plunge as into a mother-sea or reservoir . . . Not only psychic research, but metaphysical philosophy and speculative biology are led in their own ways to look with favour on some such 'panpsychic' view of the universe as this'.[11] In certain exceptional states the ordinary threshold of consciousness is lowered so that we become aware of what is contained or going on in this surrounding mother-sea of consciousness, the super mind or minds, since there might be more than one mother-sea. He employed this mother-sea hypothesis to explain his 1906 mystical experience in which he seemingly became aware of mental states not his own – free-floating states within this surrounding consciousness. He distinguished his experiences from the full-blown mystical states he featured in *The Varieties of Religious Experience* by pointing out that 'in my case certain special directions only, in the field of reality, seemed to get suddenly uncovered, whereas in classical mystical experiences it appears rather as if the whole of reality were uncovered at once'.[12]

There are some outstanding difficulties with this inference to the best explanation for the objectivity of mystical experiences. The subconscious is far too motley a crew of odd-ball states and actions to warrant an inference to the objectivity of any given subconscious state or experience. Some of them are plainly noncognitive, such as hysteria, which James also assigned to the subconscious, while others, such as hypnotism and a secondary self's perceptions, are explicable in terms of ordinary sensory ways of gaining, though not processing, information, there being no need to postulate a surrounding mother-sea of consciousness containing free-floating bits of consciousness.

James favours the pluralistic interpretation of the mother-sea of consciousness hypothesis, so that there is not a single all encompassing surrounding sea of consciousness but more than one, with God merely being the most outstanding of them in terms of power, knowledge and goodness, but still only finite. In a mystical experience, according to the surrounding mother-seas hypothesis, the subject becomes unified with one of these super consciousnesses in a way that falls short of becoming literally numerically one and the same with it but rather in the weaker sense of becoming cognizant that it is a *part* of this enveloping consciousness. This inclusion of one consciousnesses self within another raises several problems, the least of which is the one that worried James concerning how one conscious state can be a part of another.

To begin with, the idea of an individual being a proper part of another individual of the same kind is troublesome. Aristotle argued, successfully in my opinion, that no *substance*, in his special sense, could be a proper part of another substance of the same *natural kind*: A human organism, for example, cannot be a proper part of another human organism. Aristotle would not have felt challenged by a doggy door, which is a proper part of another functioning door, because a door is an *artifact* and therefore not a *substance* in his sense.

But what about a self or mind? Is it a substance and thereby subject to Aristotle's stricture? James, however, did not treat the self as a not a natural kind, because he did not leave it up to science to determine its identity conditions and therefore its nature. Maybe it is possible, after all, for a Jamesian self, understood as a succession of mental states in which the later members remember the earlier ones, to be a proper part of another self. Be that as it may, there remains the question whether it is possible for a *person*, understood as a morally responsible agent – one who performs intentional actions for which she is morally praised or blamed – to be a proper part of another person. That such a person is not a natural kind does not settle the matter in the affirmative.

James, judging by the following rhetorical question in 'The Miller-Bode Objection' notes, favoured an affirmative answer: 'Why can't I have another being own and use me, just as I am, for its purposes without knowing any of these purposes myself'.[13] This goes along with his remark that 'If we assume a wider thinker, it is evident that his purposes envelope mine. I am really lecturing *for* him'.[14] Maybe James had in mind only a case in which one person is another person's lackey or gofer, rather than one that involves actual inclusion within this person, but the text does not favour this weak rendering of his inclusion doctrine.

I believe that this doctrine is conceptually absurd for the following reason. A person, in virtue of being morally responsible for certain of her actions, must be an autonomous unit, it being the whole person, and only that person, that is held responsible for them. The reason for the 'only that person' qualification is that, according to James's Libertarianism, a morally responsible action is done freely and it is done freely only if the agent is the sole cause of it, which rules out there being another person who is responsible for the action. But if one person were a proper part of another person, both persons would be morally responsible for an intentional action performed by the former one, which is absurd according to James's libertarianism.

A deeper understanding of this absurdity can be acquired by taking seriously the common occurrence in grade school when one person would punch another and say, 'I didn't do it, my hand did'. Since the hand that delivers the punch is to be held morally responsible, it constitutes the *entire* body of the person who intentionally does the punching and does so even though it is a proper physical part of a human organism. The person whose body is entirely constituted by this human organism is supposed not to be morally responsible for delivering the punch. But if the person whose body is entirely constituted by the hand is a proper part of the person whose body is entirely constituted by the human organism, then both persons are morally responsible for the same act of delivering the punch. And this is the very absurdity in question, assuming that the act is free and we accept James's Libertarianism.

That one *person* cannot be part of another person undercuts the major attraction that pluralistic mysticism had over monistic mysticism for James. For it was in order to save the moral agency of the mystic that he felt compelled to reject all forms of monism, whether it be that of absolute idealism or monistic mysticism. But it is just this moral agency that must be sacrificed by his pluralistic mystic. There is another reason for James's mystic having to give up being a moral agent, namely that in order to have a mystical experience it is required that one overcome one's active self, which is the moral agent self, and adopt a passive attitude towards the world. Complete or partial absorption in or unification with an enveloping supernatural consciousness is alright, but the price of admission is to cease being a person – a moral agent. This is a big price for James's promethean self to pay since what is most dear to its heart is its functioning as a morally responsible agent.

Notes

1 All references to this book will be placed within parentheses in the body of the paper and are from *The Works of William James* (Cambridge: Harvard University Press edition, 1985). All subsequent quotations from James are from *The Works of William James.*
2 *Principles of Psychology*, 1181.
3 *Essays in Religion and Morality*, 128.

4   *Ibid.*

5   *A Pluralistic Universe*, 138.

6   This is worked out in the chapter on 'The Perception of Reality' in *The Principles of Psychology*. For a full discussion of the clashes between James's pragmatism and mysticism, see my book, *The Divided Self of William James* (Cambridge: Cambridge University Press, 1999).

7   William Alston, *Perceiving God: The Epistemology of Religious Experience* (Ithaca, NY: Cornell University Press, 1991); William Wainwright, *Mysticism, A Study of Its Nature, Cognitive Value, and Moral Implications* (Madison: University of Wisconsin Press, 1981); Gary Guting, *Religious Belief and Religious Skepticism* (Notre Dame, Ind.: University of Notre Dame Press, 1982); Jerome Gellman, *Experience of God and the Rationality of Theistic Belief* (Ithaca, NY: Cornell University Press, 1997), and *Mystical Experience of God* (Aldershot: Ashgate, 2001); Richard Swinburne, *The Existence of God* (Oxford: The Clarendon Press, 1991).

8   For a full discussion of this see my *On the Nature and Existence of God* (Cambridge: Cambridge University Press, 1991).

9   *A Pluralistic Universe*, 62.

10 James's four defining conditions also suffer from being too broad, since a sensation of a yellow patch, which obviously is not a mystical experience, would have to count as one.

11 *Essays in Psychical Research*, 374.

12 *Essays in Psychology*, 160.

13 *Manuscript Essays and Notes*, 129.

14 *Essays in Radical Empiricism*, 89.

CHAPTER 8

PASCAL AND THE WAGER[1]

Jeff Jordan

Blasé Pascal (1623–1662), a French polymath, is best known within the philosophy of religion for his wager in support of theistic belief.[2] As we will see there are four versions of the wager within the concise paragraphs of the *Pensées* (but throughout this essay we'll often talk as if there were only one).[3] Before looking at the various versions of the wager, let's get an idea regarding the kind of argument Pascal invented with his wager in the seventeenth century. The wager is a pragmatic argument. Pragmatic arguments for theism are designed to motivate and support belief even in the absence of strong evidential support. These arguments seek to show that theistic belief is permissible, even if one does not think that it is likely that God exists. Pragmatic arguments employ prudential reasons on behalf of their conclusions. A prudential reason for a proposition is a reason to think that believing that proposition would be beneficial. Other theistic arguments – the Ontological Proof or the Cosmological Argument for example – provide epistemic reasons in support of theism. An epistemic reason for a certain proposition is a reason to think that that proposition is true or likely. An epistemic reason is evidence. According to Pascal, if the evidence is inconclusive, one can properly consult prudence: 'your reason is not hurt by choosing one rather than the other, since you do have to make the choice. . . . But your beatitude [happiness]? Let us weigh up the gain and the loss by calling heads that God exists' (154). Theistic belief, because of its prudential benefits, defeats its rivals of atheism and agnosticism.

The four members of the family of Pascalian wagers share two characteristics. The first is that Pascal's wagers have the structure of gambles, a decision made in the midst of uncertainty. Pascal assumed that a person, just by virtue of being in the world, is in a betting situation such that one cannot avoid betting one's life on whether there is or is not a god. The wager concerning God is forced, one might say, since trying to avoid wagering is tantamount to wagering for one of the alternatives. The upshot of the wager is that one must either wager for or against the existence of God. Those are the two alternatives one unavoidably faces. To wager that God exists is to take steps to inculcate theistic belief. To wager against is to do nothing. Bringing about belief is not an action that one can directly will but one can take steps to try to bring about belief indirectly. Having acknowledged that wagering for should be understood as taking steps to bring about belief, for convenience's sake, we'll talk of believing or not believing.

If one wagers on God and believes, then there are two possible outcomes. Either God exists and one enjoys an eternity of bliss; or, God does not exist and one loses little, if anything. On the other hand, if one bets against God and wins, one gains little. But if one loses that wager, the consequences may be dismal. Because the first alternative has an outcome that overwhelms any possible gain attached to non-belief, the choice is clear says Pascal. Even if epistemic reason does not provide an answer, prudential reason does – one should try to believe. There is everything to gain and little, if anything, to lose.

And this leads to the second characteristic: a Pascalian wager is a decision situation in which the possible gain or benefit associated with at least one of the alternatives swamps all the others. As Nicolas Rescher notes with the swamping property of the wager 'agreement on the exact size of values is wholly unnecessary . . . All that matters is the rough and ready consideration that the magnitude of the value of the heavenly alternative is "incomparably greater" than that of the mundane'.[4] The gain is so great, that is, as to render the probability assignments, even if they are known, virtually irrelevant.

Before looking at the four Pascalian siblings, a brief comment on the apologetic role Pascal intended for his wagers is our first task.

The apologetic role of the wager

The *Pensées* is a collection of unfinished arguments and observations and notes that Pascal intended to draft into an apologetic for Christianity, but death prevented his ever finishing. I think it is likely that Pascal intended the wager as an argument for the rationality of theistic belief, and not as an argument especially for the rationality of Christian belief. Theism is the proposition that there exists an all powerful, all knowing, morally perfect being. Judaism, Christianity and Islam are all theistic religions. Pascal probably intended a two-step apologetic strategy in the *Pensées*. The first step would consist of arguments in support of theism generally with the wager as the clincher. The second step would consist of arguments for Christianity in particular (appeals to fulfilled prophecy and miracles were Pascal's favoured arguments in support of Christianity). Put another way, argue first that theism was rationally mandatory, and then argue that Christianity was the particular sort of theism to prefer.

If this speculation is sound, Pascal's apology was very much in line with the standard seventeenth and eighteenth century apologetic strategy – argue first that there is a divine being, and then identify which god it is that exists. This is the strategy adopted by Robert Boyle (1627–1691) and by Bishop John Tillotson (1630–1694) for instance, and by those, like William Paley (1734–1805), who employed the design argument to argue for a divine designer, and then used the argument from miracles to identify that designer.[5]

The Wagers[6]

About a third of the way into *Pensées* #680 a dialogue commences. Along with most commentators I assume that Pascal formulates his wager arguments in response to questions and comments from an unnamed interlocutor.

Prior to presenting his wager arguments Pascal sets the stage by asserting that neither the nature nor existence of God admits of rational proof, 'Reason cannot decide anything . . . Reason cannot make you choose one way or the other, reason cannot make you defend either of two choices' (153). This should not be taken as asserting that evidence and argument are irrelevant to philosophical theology. Pascal did not think that, as he clearly thought that his wager arguments were not only relevant but also rationally compelling. The wager presupposes a distinction between (A) a proposition being rational to believe, and (B) inducing a belief in that proposition being the rational thing to do.

Although a particular proposition may lack sufficient epistemic support, it could be, given the distinction between (A) and (B), that forming a belief in the proposition may be the rational thing, all things considered, to do. Pascal probably did not intend to limit the dialectical force of the wager to pragmatic rationality only. The upshot of the wager, if sound, is that belief in God is the rational stance all things considered.

Let's distinguish between something being rationally compelling and something being plausible. An argument is rationally compelling if, upon grasping the argument, one would be irrational in failing to accept its conclusion. On the other hand, an argument is plausible if, upon grasping the argument, one would be reasonable or rational in accepting its conclusion, yet one would not be irrational in failing to accepting it. Pascal believed that his wager made theistic belief rationally compelling.

Be that as it may, Ian Hacking in his important 1972 paper 'The Logic of Pascal's Wager' identifies three versions, within the *Pensées* fragments.[7] The first, which Hacking dubs the 'Argument from Dominance' is conveyed within Pascal's admonition to:

> . . . weigh up the gain and the loss by calling that heads that God exists . . . If you win, you win everything; if you lose, you lose nothing. Wager that he exists then, without hesitating. (154)

Rational optimization requires adopting a particular alternative among several mutually exclusive and jointly exhaustive options, whenever doing so may render one better-off than by not doing so, and in no case could doing so render one worse-off. According to Pascal theistic belief dominates.[8] Consider:

	God exists	~(God exists)[9]
Believe[10]	F1	F2
~(Believe)	F3	F4

In this matrix there are two states of the world (possible ways that the world might be), one in which God exists and one in which God does not exist; and two alternatives (actions or choices available to the agent), whether to bring about belief or not.[11] Given that the outcomes associated with the alternatives have the following relations: F1 >> F3, and F2 is at least as good as F4, belief weakly dominates not believing.[12] Following Pascal, no great disvalue has been assigned to F3. Nowhere in *Pensées* #680 does Pascal suggest that non-belief results in hell, or an infinite disutility, if God exists.

Represented schematically the argument from dominance proceeds:

1. For any person S, if one of the alternatives, α, available to S has an outcome better than the outcomes of the other available alternatives, and never an outcome worse than the others, S should choose α. And,
2. believing in God is better than not believing if God exists, and is no worse if God does not exist. Therefore,
C. one should believe in God.

This first wager is an example of a decision under uncertainty. Whenever one deliberates with knowledge of the outcomes but no knowledge of the probabilities associated with those outcomes, one faces a decision under uncertainty. On the other hand, if one deliberates armed with knowledge of both the outcomes and the probabilities associated with those outcomes, one faces a decision under risk.

The transition to the second version of the wager is precipitated by the interlocutor's objection to the assumption that theistic wagering does not render one worse-off if God does not exist. In response Pascal introduces probability assignments to the discussion, and, more importantly, the idea of an infinite utility:

> Since there is an equal chance of gain and loss, if you won only two lives instead of one, you could still put on a bet. But if there were three lives to win, you would have to play . . . and you would be unwise . . . not to chance your life to win three in a game where there is an equal chance of losing and winning. (154)

While probability plays no part in the first argument, it has a prominent role in the second version of the wager, which Hacking calls the 'Argument from Expectation'. Built upon the concept of maximizing expected utility the argument from expectation assumes that the probability that God exists is one-half, and that the outcome of right belief, if God exists, is of infinite utility.[13] With these assumptions theistic belief easily outdistances not believing, no matter what finite value is found in F2, F3 or F4:

	God exists $1/_2$	~(God exists) $1/_2$	
Believe	0.5, ∞	0.5, F2	EU = ∞
~(Believe)	0.5, F3	0.5, F4	EU = finite value

Put schematically:

3. For any person S, and alternatives, α and β, available to S, if α has a greater expected utility than does β, S should choose α. And,
4. given that the existence of God is as likely as not, believing in God carries more expected utility than does not believing. Therefore,
C. one should believe in God.

Hacking asserts that the assumption of equal chance is 'monstrous'. Perhaps it is. The beautiful thing about infinite utility, though, is that infinity multiplied by any finite value is still infinite.[14] The assumption that the existence of God is just as likely as not is needlessly extravagant, since, as long as the probability of the existence of God is judged to be greater than zero, believing will always carry an expected utility greater than that carried by non-belief. And this is true no matter the value or disvalue associated with the outcomes F2, F3 and F4. This observation underlies the third version of the wager, what Hacking titles the 'Argument from Dominating Expectation' in which p represents a positive probability, with a range greater than zero and less than one-half:

	God exists, p $1/_2$	~(God exists), 1–p $1/_2$	
Believe	p, ∞	1–p, F2	EU = ∞
~(Believe)	p, F3	1–p, F4	EU = finite value

No matter how unlikely it is that God exists, as long as there is some positive non-zero probability that he does, believing is one's best bet:

5. For any person S, and alternatives, α and β, available to S, if α has a greater expected utility than does β, S should choose α. And,
6. believing in God has a greater expected utility than does not believing. Therefore,
C. one should believe in God.

Because of its ingenious employment of infinite utility, the third version has become what most philosophers think of as Pascal's wager. It is the canonical version. Even so, the argument from dominating expectation is not Pascal's most formidable.

The fourth version of the wager found in *Pensées* #680 resides in the concluding remarks that Pascal makes to his interlocutor:

> But what harm will come to you from taking this course? You will be faithful, honest, humble, grateful, doing good, a sincere and true friend. It is, of course, true; you will not take part in corrupt pleasure, in glory, in the pleasures of high living. But will you not have others?
> I tell you that you will win thereby in this life . . . (156)

The fourth version brings us full circle, away from arguments under risk and back to an argument under uncertainty.[15] This version remedies the defect that precluded the first argument from strict dominance.

	God exists	~(God exists)
Believe	∞	F2
~(Believe)	F3	F4

Like, its predecessors the fourth version implies that the benefits of belief vastly exceed those of non-belief if God exists; but, unlike the others, the fourth implies that F2 > F4. No matter what, belief is one's best bet. Belief strictly dominates non-belief. Let's call this version of the wager the 'Argument from Strict Dominance':

7. For any person S, if among the alternatives available to S, the outcomes of one alternative, α, are better in every state than those of the other available alternatives, and the states are causally independent of the available actions, S should choose α. And,
8. believing in God is better than not believing whether God exists or not. Therefore,
C. one should believe in God.

Premise (8) is true only if one gains simply by believing. Importantly, (8) should not be understood as asserting that one can have good reason to hold that there is no divine reality, and yet one can believe in God. Premise (8) is saying that even when shrouded in the fog of epistemic uncertainty of whether there is a God or not, there is still practical benefit to theistic belief. Pascal apparently thought that this was obvious. Sincere theistic belief results, he thought, in virtuous living and virtuous living is more rewarding than vicious living.

The response of Pascal's interlocutor, we might plausibly imagine, would be that Pascal has made an illicit assumption: why think that virtuous living requires theism? And even if virtuous living requires theism, why think that being morally better is tantamount to being better-off all things considered? Now whether virtue is its own reward only in a theistic context or not, the relevant point is whether theistic belief provides more benefit than not believing, even if we lack strong evidence that God exists. If it does, then this is an important point when considering the many-gods objection.

The many-Gods objection

Notice that in all four Pascalian arguments the wager consists of a 2 × 2 matrix: there are two acts available to the agent, with only two possible states of the world. From Pascal's day to this, critics have been quick to point out that Pascal's partitioning of the possible states of the world overlooks the obvious – what if some deity other than the theistic one exists?[16] What if a deity exists that harbours animus towards theism? In effect, the many-gods objection asserts that Pascal's 2 × 2 matrix is flawed because the states it employs are not jointly exhaustive of the possibilities.

To understand the many-gods objection let's expand the 2×2 matrix into a 3×3 one, adding the existence of a non-theistic deity as a possible state of the world:

	G	N	D
Believe in G	∞ F1	F2	F3
Believe in Neither	F4	F5	∞ F6
Believe in D	F7	F8	∞ F9

With D representing the existence of a non-theistic deity, a 'deviant' deity, and N representing the world with no deity of any sort (call this state 'naturalism'). Notice the 3×3 matrix is arranged such that D rewards atheists and those believing in D, but punishes theists. In this arrangement theistic belief no longer strictly dominates. Indeed, with an infinite utility residing in all both columns G and D, and, with the values of F3, F4 and F7 presumably the same, even weak dominance seems lost to theism. The upshot of the many-gods objection is that the wager provides no pragmatic support for theism, so the Pascalian has no good reason to prefer theism over even a gerrymandered fictional 'deviant deity', let alone naturalism, once the decision situation is expanded as a 3×3 matrix.

Our construction of the 3×3 matrix employs a deviant deity – an instance of what we might, albeit tendentiously, term a 'philosophers' fiction' – a deity or religion imaginatively described by a philosopher, usually in the course of criticizing the wager, which is not tied to any historical religion. The employment of philosophers' fictions seems de rigueur for contemporary proponents of the many-gods objection. Richard Gale, for example, regales us with the possibility of a sidewalk crack god; while Michael Martin conjures up a perverse master of the universe who 'punishes with infinite torment after death anyone who believes in God or any other supernatural being (including himself) and rewards with infinite bliss after death anyone who believes in no supernatural being'.[17] The many-gods objection can be constructed with philosophers' fictions or with deities claimed by actual historical religions (Allah, or Yahweh, or . . .).[18] The employment of philosophers' fictions seems to bloat the Pascalian partition even greater than those employing only historical examples. But from the logical point of view the description of the third column (the D column in the 3 × 3 matrix above), whether actual or imaginary, is irrelevant. Indeed, adding columns beyond the third (4 × 4 matrix, or a 5 × 5 matrix, or a . . .), while perhaps rhetorically striking, is logically redundant to the force of the many-gods objection.

The many-gods objection's attempt to expand the Pascalian matrix from a 2 × 2 to a 3 × 3 one presents a powerful objection to the wager. Does the inflation of the Pascalian matrix devalue the wager argument beyond use? Does this objection defeat the wager?

It is far from clear that it does. Let me describe three strategies a Pascalian could employ as to defuse the many-gods objection (in effect, deflate the 3 × 3 matrix back to a 2 × 2 one). While page constraints preclude a detailed development of each strategy, I hope to say enough to indicate that the Pascalian has the resources available with which to defeat the many-gods objection.

The first strategy would argue that one could salvage from the ruins of the fourth version a wager that circumvents the many-gods objection. Given that the lower two cells of the D column in the 3 × 3 matrix equal the upper cell of the G column, and that $F3 = F4 = F7$, the Pascalian could employ proposition (8), if true, as a principled way to adjudicate between believing theistically or not. That is, whether one believes theistically, or believes in a deviant deity, or refrains from believing in any deity at all, one is exposed to the same kind of risk ($F3$ or $F4$ or $F7$), as the worst outcomes of theistic belief, of deviant belief, and of naturalistic belief are on a par. Moreover, whether one believes theistically, or believes in a deviant deity, or refrains from believing in any deity at all, one enjoys eligibility for the same kind of reward ($\infty = \infty = \infty$). The best outcomes, that is, of theistic belief, of deviant belief and of naturalistic belief are on a par. But in a situation in which we do not know whether God exists or not, it may well be that adopting theism provides a better this world (as opposed to afterlife) outcome than does adopting naturalism or theological deviance. If it is true that theists are, on average, happier than non-theists, then, everything else being equal, one has a reason to prefer theism over its rivals. This strategy works only if there is credible social science evidence that theistic belief reliably correlates with positive indicators of health and happiness.[19]

A second strategy argues that those versions of the many-gods objection which employ philosophers' fictions imply that logical possibility requires a non-zero, non-infinitesimal probability assignment. In short: logical possibility implies a positive probability. But the Pascalian could argue that logical possibility does not imply a positive probability, by noting the distinction between logical possibility and metaphysical possibility.[20] This distinction, very roughly, is between that which we can consistently describe (logical possibility), and that which is in fact possible given the metaphysical structure of reality (metaphysical possibility). To illustrate with a common example: perhaps we can imagine water being made of carbon and chlorine (logical possibility), but it may be metaphysically impossible that water be anything other than H_2O, since that is what water essentially is. In like manner, philosophers' fictions may be logically possible as we can consistently describe a perverse master of the universe deity for instance. But that is little or no reason to hold that these imaginary constructions are also metaphysically possible given what else we know about the universe. And while it may be plausible that positive probability flows from metaphysical possibility, it is doubtful that it flows from logical possibility alone. The utility of this strategy is limited to those versions of the many-gods objection employing philosophers' fictions.

A third strategy open to the Pascalian builds upon a distinction introduced by William James in his 1894 essay, 'The Will to Believe'.[21] There James distinguished between live hypotheses and dead ones:

> Let us give the name of hypothesis to anything that may be proposed to our belief; and just as the electricians speak of live and dead wires, let us speak of any hypothesis as either live or dead. A live hypothesis is one which appeals as a real possibility to him to whom it is proposed. If I ask you to believe in the Mahdi, the notion makes no electric connection with your nature, – it refuses to scintillate with any credibility at all. As an hypothesis it is completely dead. To an Arab, however (even if he be not one of the Madhi's followers), the hypothesis is among the mind's possibilities: it is alive. This shows that deadness and liveness in an hypothesis are not intrinsic properties, but relations to the individual thinker. They are measured by his willingness to act. The maximum of liveness in hypothesis means willingness to act irrevocably. Practically, that means belief; but there is some believing tendency wherever there is willingness to act at all.[22]

James says that a hypothesis is live just in case one is willing to act upon it. Instead of James's term 'hypothesis' let's talk of alternatives (what one can choose in a decision situation). We might tighten the notion of a live alternative by saying that an alternative is live for a person just in case that person lacks strong evidence disconfirming the state relevant for that particular alternative, and the alternative has an intuitive appeal for that person, and adopting the alternative involves no significant opportunity costs. Importantly, the liveliness of alternatives is person-relative. An alternative alive for you may not be for me, though presumably the range of live alternatives will be shared by those situated in similar intellectual and social contexts. James recognized that those similarly situated likely shared the same set of live alternatives (or what he called 'options'), when he said 'If I say to you: "Be a theosophist or be a Mohammedan," it is probably a dead option, because for you neither hypothesis is likely to be alive. But if I say: "Be an agnostic or be Christian," it is otherwise: trained as you are, each hypothesis makes some appeal, however small, to your belief'.[23]

With the Jamesian distinction between live and dead alternatives in hand the Pascalian can credibly reject philosophers' fictions and many historical deities as dead alternatives – alternatives that receive a zero probability assignment. So, return to the 3 × 3 matrix above. One could reasonably reject the last alternative (believe in D) as dead – perhaps the opportunity costs of believing in D are too high, or perhaps the fact that D is a philosophers' fiction puts it beyond credibility. That is, one could reasonably hold that the probability that a deviant deity exists are, practically speaking, nil. And it is not implausible to think that the same would hold for however one describes the third column, whether involving a philosophers' fiction or an exotic actual religion, since it would not be surprising that the vast majority of those who encounter the wager are in the position described by James: 'if I say: "Be an agnostic or be Christian", . . . trained as you are, each hypothesis makes some appeal, however small, to your belief'.

Is Pascalian wagering immoral?

There is a widespread and influential tradition found in Western philosophy, a tradition that we can call 'evidentialism', which holds that:

> E. for all persons S and propositions P, it is permissible for S to believe that P only if P is supported by adequate evidence.

With regard to any proposition that one entertains, a person will stand in one of four doxastic states. One will either believe that the proposition is more likely than not, or one will believe that the proposition is less likely than not, or one will believe that it is just as likely as not, or one will have no belief concerning the likelihood of the proposition. According to (E), one should believe a proposition only if one finds oneself in the first doxastic state. Endorsing (E) many philosophers have held that pragmatic reasons for belief-formation are illegitimate since such reasons do not themselves provide adequate evidence for the truth of the belief. Perhaps the most-quoted statement of the evidentialist imperative is that of W. K. Clifford (1845–1879): 'it is wrong always, everywhere, and for any one, to believe anything upon insufficient evidence'.[24] Clifford fashioned (E) in a moral sense: it is morally impermissible to believe something lacking the support of sufficient evidence. The normative sense of (E) can also be understood as a cognitive standard: it is irrational to believe in the absence of sufficient evidence. Whether moral or cognitive, does (E) present an insurmountable obstacle to Pascal's wager? The first thing to ask is whether (E) is even true. A promising argument that (E) is in fact false is:

9. No one is ever irrational in doing what one is morally obligated to do.[27] And,
10. inculcating a belief in a certain proposition, even when that proposition lacks the support of sufficient evidence, could be a moral obligation. Therefore,
11. inculcating a belief even with the lack of sufficient evidence could be rational.[25]

Is (9) plausible? In chapter XV of the *Leviathan* Thomas Hobbes (1588–1679) famously describes one who would doubt it:

The Foole hath sayd in his heart, there is no such thing as Justice; and sometimes also with his tongue; seriously alleaging, that every mans conservation, and contentment, being committed to his own care, there could be no reason, why every man might not do what he thought conduced thereunto: and therefore also to make, or not make; keep, or not keep Covenants, was not against Reason, when it conduced to ones benefit. He does not therein deny, that there be Covenants; and that they are sometimes broken, sometimes kept; and that such breach of them may be called Injustice, and the observance of them Justice; but he questioneth, whether Injustice, taking away the feare of God, (for the same Foole hath said in his heart there is no God), may not sometimes stand with that Reason, which dictateth to every man his own good; and particularly then, when it conduceth to such a benefit, as revilings, but also the power of other men.[26]

Since this is no place to argue against Hobbes' Fool I will simply note that others have offered impressive answers to the Fool; and these answers, I believe, render (9) plausible.[27]

In support of (10) we will employ a case in which one has a moral obligation to bring about a belief, and yet lacks adequate evidence that the belief is true. Consider:

> Jones knows that expecting an event to be painful is correlated strongly with an increase in the intensity of felt pain (as opposed to having no expectation, or expecting the event to be relatively painless). Her son is about to have a boil lanced. Jones believes that she is morally obligated to minimize pain and she desires to minimize her son's suffering as much as possible. Knowing that her son will trust her, Jones tells him that the procedure will be relatively painless. She does so even though she lacks evidence that such procedures are in fact typically painless.

It is clear that Jones has done nothing wrong in bringing about her son's belief that the lancing will be relatively painless. Our judgement that Jones is in the clear, morally and rationally, in her actions is support for premise (10). Moreover, if one can be in the moral and rational clear with inculcating a belief in others that lacks sufficient evidence; one could likewise be in the clear in doing so with regard to oneself.

One might object that the argument fails since it is valid only if a proposition like the following is true:

> G. if S is justified in doing things that will result in her doing x, then S is justified in doing x.

But one might argue that (G) is false. For instance, one might allege that the following is a counterexample to (G):

> Suppose an evil and powerful tyrant offers me the following choice: die now, or submit to an irreversible and irresistible hypnotic suggestion which will cause

me to kill myself five years from now. I have no other option. Surely I am practically justified in submitting to hypnosis in these circumstances. But it would be bizarre to maintain that five years from now, I am practically justified in killing myself.[28]

If (G) is false, and if the argument relies on (G), then we have a strong objection contra the argument (9–11).

But the evil tyrant case is no counterexample to proposition (G). Proposition (G) is specifically about actions. Irreversible and irresistible events that happen to one are not actions of that person. In the alleged counterexample one's killing oneself is not an action (there is no deliberation or choice involved), it is an unavoidable consequence of gaining an additional five years of life. Of course the failure of this attack on proposition (G) does not entail that it is true, but given its intuitive appeal there is reason to accept (G). So, even if (G) is pre-supposed by (9–11), we've as yet no reason to doubt it.

Premises (9) and (10), clearly enough, entail (11). Hence, (E) is false. But, importantly, the falsity of (E) does not warrant a promiscuous deployment of Pascalian wagers. For one thing, one could argue that Pascalian wagers are properly employed only when the evidence is balanced or inconclusive. That is, one might argue that the wager is properly a tie-breaker when one takes the evidence that God exists and the con-evidence to be more or less balanced. As Pascal put this point: 'your reason suffers no more violence in choosing one rather than the other'. But if there is reason to think that evidence might be forth-coming, suspending judgement might be the rational thing to do, at least for a time. Perhaps a more modest form of evidentialism can be salvaged, but it cannot take on Cliffordian proportions. Modest evidentialism would hold that when the evidence speaks, one must listen. If the evidence supports P, then one may be rationally obligated to accept P. But if the evidence is indeterminate regarding P – it is just as likely as not – one may on pragmatic grounds accept or reject P. Modest evidentialism understood this way is a defeasible rule operative under normal conditions. That is, while (E) is false, perhaps (E') is true:

E'. for all persons S and propositions P, S is obligated to believe that P if P is supported by adequate evidence.

A Pascalian can accept (E′), as it presents to no challenge to a use of the wager in those cases in which it is employed as a tie-breaker. So, is Pascalian wagering immoral? There's reason to think not.

In conclusion

Based on the preceding arguments we cannot say that the wager escapes every possible objection, since philosophers are a clever bunch, perhaps an objection, as yet not conceived, but more powerful than any yet presented might be produced. But until that day, we are in a position to say that the wager eludes the two objections usually considered the most serious, and that result should give the Pascalian hope. All in all, then, as things stand, we can say that even if no one has conclusive evidence that God exists, it is clear that there is strong pragmatic reason to wager that he does.

Notes

1 Some of the material is revised and adapted from my book, *Pascal's Wager: Pragmatic arguments and belief in God* (Oxford: Clarendon Press, 2006).

2 For details concerning Pascal's life and his work outside of the wager, see the various essays found in *The Cambridge Companion to Pascal*, (ed.) N. Hammond (Cambridge: Cambridge University Press, 2003).

3 *Pensées*, trans. by Honor Levi, (Oxford: Oxford University Press, 1995), 153–6. In the Levi translation the relevant passage is #680. All *Pensées* page citations are hereafter cited in the text, and are to the Levi edition.

4 Nicholas Rescher, *Pascal's Wager: A study of practical reasoning in philosophical theology* (Notre Dame, IN: Notre Dame University Press, 1985), 20.

5 On Boyle see *Final Causes of Natural Things* (1688); on Tillotson see 'The Wisdom of Being Religious' Sermon I, *Works of Tillotson*, Vol. I (London: J. F. Dove, 1820), 317–89; and see Paley's *A View of the Evidences of Christianity* (1795), Part 3, chapter 8.

6 For more detail on the various versions of the wager see, in addition to Hacking, Edward McClennen, 'Pascal's Wager and Finite Decision Theory', in *Gambling on God: Essays on Pascal's Wager* (Lanham, MD: Rowman & Littlefield, 94), 115–37. And see Alan Hájek, 'The Illogic of Pascal's Wager' *Proceedings of the 10th Logica International Symposium*, Liblice, (ed.) T. Childers et al., 239–49.

7 'The Logic of Pascal's Wager' *American Philosophical Quarterly* 9/2 (1972), 186–92.

8 As described, the first version of the wager is an argument from *weak* dominance – believing in God is better than the other alternatives in at least one state and no worse in any state.

9 Understanding God as that individual, if any, who is omnipotent, omniscient and morally perfect.

10 While it may be better to understand the alternatives as (taking steps to bring about belief in God), and not-(taking steps to bring about belief in God), for convenience, I will formulate the alternatives as simply (*Believe*) and ~(*Believe*).

11 A matrix is a way of representing a decision situation. It involves:

States

Alternatives   Outcomes

- Alternatives = ways of acting available to the deliberator.
- States = ways the world might be.
- Outcomes = consequences or results of the actions in the various states.

The number of outcomes within a matrix (call the little boxes 'cells') is a function of the number of states multiplied by the number of alternatives.

12 The expression $X \gg Y$ should be understood as X *greatly exceeds* Y. The alternatives in this case have no propensity to bring about the states – they are causally and logically independent.

13 One calculates the expected utility of an act φ by (i) multiplying the benefits and probabilities of each outcome associated with φ, (ii) subtracting any respective costs, (iii) summing the totals from each associated outcome. So, the expected utility of believing in God, given an infinite utility and 0.5 probabilities, is: $(\infty \times \frac{1}{2}) + (F2 \times \frac{1}{2}) = \infty$.

14 Assuming, plausibly enough, that no sense can be made in this context of infinitesimal probabilities.

15 Edward McClennen has suggested that another version of the wager employing only finite utilities and something like the principle of indifference is also contained in #680. See McClennen, 'Pascal's Wager and Finite Decision Theory', 127–9.

16 The number of critics invoking the many-gods objection is legion. Among their number are Paul Saka, 'Pascal's Wager and the Many-Gods Objection' *Religious Studies* 37 (2001), 321–41; Graham Priest, *Logic: A Very Short Introduction* (Oxford: Oxford UP, 2000), 94–8; William Gustason, 'Pascal's Wager and Competing Faiths' *International Journal for Philosophy of Religion* 44 (1998), 31–9; Richard Gale, *On The Nature And Existence of God* (NY: Cambridge University Press, 1991), 349–51; Antony Flew, 'Is Pascal's Wager the Only Safe Bet?' *God, Freedom and Immortality* (Buffalo, NY: Prometheus, 1984), 61–8; Michael Martin, 'Pascal's

Wager as an Argument for not Believing in God' *Religious Studies* 19 (1983), 57–64; J. L. Mackie, *The Miracle of Theism* (Oxford: Clarendon, 1982), 203; Peter Dalton, 'Pascal's Wager: The Second Argument' *Southern Journal of Religion* 13 (1975), 31–46; Merle Turner, 'Deciding for God – the Bayesian Support of Pascal's Wager' *Philosophy and Phenomenological Research* 29/1 (1968), 84–90; and James Cargile, 'Pascal's Wager' *Philosophy* 41 (1966), 250–7.

17 Richard Gale, *On the Nature And Existence of God*, 349–51. Michael Martin, *Atheism: A Philosophical Justification* (Philadelphia: Temple University Press, 1990), 232–4.

18 The early formulations of the many-gods objection typically employed Islam as the third column. Today, philosophers' fictions are typically employed.

19 See, for instance, Ralph W. Hood, Jr., Bernard Spilka, Bruce Hunsberger and Richard Gorsuch, *The Psychology of Religion* (NY: Guilford Press, 1996, 2nd edition), 384. And, David Lykken, *Happiness* (New York: St. Martin's Press, 1999), 18–19. And, Harold Koenig, Michael McCullough, and David Larson, *Handbook of Religion and Health* (Oxford: Oxford University Press, 2001), 117, 215–5. And, M. E. Cullough, W. T. Hoyt, D. Larsen, H. G. Koenig and C. E. Thoresen, 'Religious Involvement and Mortality: A Meta-analytic Review' *Health Psychology* 19 (2000), 211–22.

20 See Saul Kripke, 'Naming and Necessity' in *Semantics of Natural Language*, ed. Donald Davidson and Gilbert Harmon (Dordrecht: D. Reidel Pub. Co, 1972).

21 'The Will to Believe' in *The Will To Believe and Other Essays in Popular Philosophy* (NY: Dover, 1956), 1–31.

22 James, 'Will to Believe', 2–3.

23 James, 'Will to Believe', 3.

24 W. K. Clifford, 'The Ethics of Belief' in *Lectures and Essays*, Vol. II (London: Macmillan, 1879), 186.

25 It may be that (9–11) should be revised to read:

9'. No one is ever (overall) irrational in doing what one is morally obligated to do. And,

10. inculcating a belief in a certain proposition, even when that proposition lacks the support of sufficient evidence, could be a moral obligation. Therefore,

11'. inculcating a belief even with the lack of sufficient evidence could be (overall) rational.

The locutions '(overall) rational' and '(overall) irrational' presuppose that there are various kinds of rationality, including moral rationality, epistemic rationality and prudential rationality. The idea that there are various kinds of rationality recognizes that at any time one could have conflicting obligations. One might be obligated to do various things, doing all of which it's not possible to do. Overall rationality is the all-things-considered perspective. It is what one ultimately should do; having taken into account the various obligations one is under at a particular time. Overall rationality, or all-things-considered rationality (ATC rationality), is, in W. D. Ross's terms, one's actual duty in the particular circumstances, even if one has other conflicting *prima facie* duties. As revised, the argument assumes that if in doing something one is not ATC irrational, then it follows that one is ATC rational in doing it.

The argument could also revised without presupposing that there are various kinds of rationality, by replacing the principle that no one is ever irrational in doing her moral duty, with the principle that moral obligations take precedence whenever a conflict of obligations occurs.

26 Thomas Hobbes, *Leviathan* (1651; reprint: Harmondsworth: Penguin, 1968), 203.
27 See, for instance, Gregory S. Kavka, 'The Reconciliation Project' in *Morality, Reason and Truth: New Essays on the Foundation of Ethics*, eds. D. Copp and D. Zimmerman (Totowa, NJ: Rowman & Allanheld, 1985), 297–319; and his 'The Rationality of Rule-Following: Hobbes's Dispute With The Foole' *Law and Philosophy* 14 (1995), 5–34. And see the informative discussion in Owen McLeod's 'Just Plain 'Ought" *The Journal of Ethics* 5 (2001), 269–91.
28 Eugene Mills, 'The Unity of Justification' *Philosophy and Phenomenological Research* 58 (1998), 34–5.

CHAPTER 9

HUME AND REPORTS OF MIRACLES
David Johnson

Hume, Holism and Miracles[1] seems to have excited a murmur among the zealots. Robert Fogelin, for example, has said a variety of nasty things about my 'misguided, often ill-tempered, bashing'[2] of Hume's essay. I think it is fair to say that the fate of revealed religion turns on the merits of Hume's essay, and that the interpretation of the essay turns on the controversy between Fogelin and me. I shall begin by considering Fogelin's characterization of Hume's reasoning. I shall find that characterization wanting, and then turn to Hume's actual reasoning.[3]

What Fogelin calls 'Hume's argument concerning miracles – specifically concerning religious miracles' (30) is, putting it in Fogelinesque terms, surely something along the following lines:

1. 'The standards for testimony establishing' a miracle 'must be extremely high'.
2. No testimony to a religious miracle has ever met standards that are 'extremely high'.

   Therefore:

3. No testimony to a religious miracle has ever established (the occurrence of) that miracle.

Fogelin purports to find in part 1 of Hume's essay a 'central argument' (67) for (1), but that argument is never stated by Fogelin with anything resembling rigour. His remarks on the subject are best construed as being allusions to some Bayesian argument; an argument which, if stated seriously, would be subject to the critique given in the

Chapter 7 of my book, a critique which Fogelin ignores. Thus I shall not dwell on what he says. There is no hint in Fogelin's book that he knows how to rescue the Bayesian Hume from his critics. For all that Fogelin (or his Hume) has *shown* to be the case, I could be justly persuaded of the occurrence of a miracle, by a postcard from a drunkard who claims to have walked on the Sea of Cortez.

Even if we had (1), on what grounds would Hume have us believe (2)? Here is the sort of thing Fogelin says:

> In short, for Hume, it is an empirical fact, amply illustrated by history, that testimony concerning religious miracles is notoriously unreliable. On the basis of this general fact about the quality of such testimony, the wise reasoner has ample grounds for rejecting it. (29)

> . . . the two parts of Hume's discussion of miracles operate in tandem. Through probabilistic reasoning [of a kind never rigorously stated or seriously examined by Fogelin], part 1 [supposedly] fixes the appropriate level of scrutiny for evaluating testimony with respect to miracles; part 2 considers the quality of the testimony that has hitherto been brought forth in support of religious miracles and concludes that it comes nowhere near to meeting the appropriate standards. More strongly, an examination of historical records shows such a consistent pattern of ignorance, deceit, and credulity that the wise reasoner is fully justified in rejecting all testimony given in support of a miracle intended to serve as the foundation of a system of religion. (31)

For Fogelin, meeting the appropriate 'extremely high' standards cannot *mean* anything about, say, the plenitude of witnesses. For he says that Hume gives an argument in part 1 for (1); if testimony's meeting 'extremely high' standards conceptually required that it be, say, the testimony of *many* (and so not merely of *one*), then Fogelin would have Hume arguing a priori (note Fogelin's 'must' in (1)) for something at least as strong as the (H) from my book![4] In the end (my limited space requires that I be very brief about this point) meeting 'extremely high' standards turns out to *mean* something like: being testimony of a kind which has usually (or almost always, or always) been found to be correct, *and* being testimony of *no* kind which has usually (or almost always, or always) been found to be incorrect. So I take it that testimony to religious miracles is supposed to have come 'nowhere near to meeting' such standards because every bit of it is of a kind – namely, *testimony to a religious miracle* – which has, supposedly, usually (or almost always, or always) been found to be incorrect; to wit: 'notoriously unreliable'.

How would Hume have learned this? Empirically, historically, Fogelin avers. Fogelin portrays Hume as being a purely historical detector of the unreliability of testimony, hitherto given, in support of religious miracles. This reading of Hume is textually indefensible. In order to see this, it is important that you have easily before your eyes a block of passages from the second part of Hume's essay. I quote from the text of that essay helpfully reprinted as an appendix in Fogelin's book, with its convenient paragraph numbers (and I later cite two other paragraphs, without quoting them in their entirety; and make other short quotations, without reference):

[31] How many stories of this nature have, in all ages, been detected and exploded in their infancy? How many more have been celebrated for a time, and have afterwards sunk into neglect and oblivion? Where such reports, therefore, fly about, the solution of the phenomenon is obvious; and we judge in conformity to regular experience and observation, when we account for it by the known and natural principles of credulity and delusion. And shall we, rather than have a recourse to so natural a solution, allow of a miraculous violation of the most established laws of nature?

[32] I need not mention the difficulty of detecting a falsehood in any private or even public history, at the place, where it is said to happen; much more when the scene is removed to ever so small a distance. Even a court of judicature, with all the authority, accuracy, and judgment, which they can employ, find themselves often at a loss to distinguish between truth and falsehood in the most recent actions. But the matter never comes to any issue, if trusted to the common method of altercation and debate and flying rumours; especially when men's passions have taken part on either side.

[33] In the infancy of new religions, the wise and learned commonly esteem the matter too inconsiderable to deserve their attention or regard. And when afterwards they would willingly detect the cheat, in order to undeceive the deluded multitude, the season is now past, and the records and witnesses, which might clear up the matter, have perished beyond recovery.

[34] No means of detection remain, but those which must be drawn from the very testimony itself of the reporters: And these, though always sufficient with the judicious and knowing, are commonly too fine to fall under the comprehension of the vulgar.

[35] Upon the whole, then, it appears, that no testimony for any kind of miracle has ever amounted to a probability, much less to a proof; and that, even supposing it

amounted to a proof, it would be opposed by another proof; derived from the very nature of the fact, which it would endeavour to establish. It is experience only, which gives authority to human testimony; and it is the same experience, which assures us of the laws of nature. When, therefore, these two kinds of experience are contrary, we have nothing to do but subtract the one from the other, and embrace an opinion, either on one side or the other, with that assurance which arises from the remainder. But according to the principle here explained, this subtraction, with regard to all popular religions, amounts to an entire annihilation; and therefore we may establish it as a maxim, that no human testimony can have such force as to prove a miracle, and make it a just foundation for any such system of religion.

[36] I beg the limitations here made may be remarked, when I say, that a miracle can never be proved, so as to be the foundation of a system of religion. For I own, that otherwise, there may possibly be miracles, or violations of the usual course of nature, of such a kind as to admit of proof from human testimony; though, perhaps, it will be impossible to find any such in all the records of history. Thus, suppose, all authors, in all languages, agree, that, from the first of January 1600, there was a total darkness over the whole earth for eight days: Suppose that the tradition of this extraordinary event is still strong and lively among the people: That all travellers, who return from foreign countries, bring us accounts of the same tradition, without the least variation or contradiction: It is evident, that our present philosophers, instead of doubting the fact, ought to receive it as certain, and ought to search for the causes whence it might be derived. The decay, corruption, and dissolution of nature, is an event rendered probable by so many analogies, that any phenomenon, which seems to have a tendency towards that catastrophe, comes within the reach of human testimony, if that testimony be very extensive and uniform.

[37] But suppose, that all the historians, who treat of England, should agree, that, on the first of January 1600, Queen Elizabeth died; that both before and after her death she was seen by her physicians and the whole court, as is usual with persons of her rank; that her successor was acknowledged and proclaimed by the parliament; and that, after being interred a month, she again appeared, resumed the throne, and governed England for three years: I must confess that I should be surprised at the concurrence of so many odd circumstances, but should not have the least inclination to believe so miraculous an event. I should not doubt of her pretended death, and of those other public circumstances that followed it: I should only assert it to have been pretended, and that it neither was, nor possibly could be real. You would in vain object to me the difficulty, and almost impossibility of deceiving the world in an affair of such consequence; the wisdom and solid judgment of that renowned queen; with the little or no advantage which she could reap from so poor an artifice: All this might astonish me; but I would still reply, that the knavery and folly of men are such common phenomena,

that I should rather believe the most extraordinary events to arise from their concurrence, than admit of so signal a violation of the laws of nature.

[38] But should this miracle be ascribed to any new system of religion; men, in all ages, have been so much imposed on by ridiculous stories of that kind, that this very circumstance would be a full proof of a cheat, and sufficient, with all men of sense, not only to make them reject the fact, but even reject it without farther examination. Though the Being, to whom the miracle is ascribed, be, in this case, Almighty, it does not, upon that account, become a whit more probable; since it is impossible for us to know the attributes or actions of such a Being, otherwise than from the experience which we have of his productions, in the usual course of nature. This still reduces us to past observation, and obliges us to compare the instances of the violations of truth in the testimony of men with those of the violations of the laws of nature by miracles, in order to judge which of them is most likely and probable. As the violations of truth are more common in the testimony concerning religious miracles, than in that concerning any other matter of fact; this must diminish very much the authority of the former testimony, and make us form a general resolution, never to lend any attention to it, with whatever specious pretence it may be covered.

Two of Hume's passages which might seem to support Fogelin (31 and 35) serve as book-ends to the long passage, 32–4, about how 'the season is now past' (for historical investigation), which passage *undermines* Fogelin's construal of Hume as a purported historical detector of the unreliability of testimony concerning religious miracles. So what is going on in passages 31–8 from part 2 of Hume's essay? Fogelin is right to think that there is *something* going on here which has to do peculiarly with testimony to *religious* miracles. But he is very wrong about what Hume is saying about such testimony. Let us look closely, and see.

The rhetorical questions at the beginning of 31 are evidently an appeal by Hume for us to agree (perhaps because it has somehow already been established?) that there has been a great unreliability attaching to reports of religious miracles – 'many instances' of 'forged miracles' and the like (as he puts it in 19). He then says 'therefore' . . . something. But 'therefore' . . . *what*? Therefore: 'Where such reports . . . fly about, the solution of the phenomenon is *obvious*' (my emphasis). Hume is saying that, since religious miracle-reports (or, at least, foundational ones) have such an unhappy track-record (the unhappiness of which is reasserted by way of the rhetorical questions), it is *obvious* what we should do when confronted by a new report of that kind.

We should reject the report as being, obviously, untrue, and 'account for it by the known and natural principles of credulity and delusion'. As Hume says in 38, we 'men of sense' will not only 'reject the fact', but 'reject it *without farther examination*' (my emphasis). Why 'without farther examination'? Because it is *obviously* untrue. (No *need* to 'trace its falsehood'.) Why is it obviously untrue? Because it is ascribed to a 'new system of religion' and (since 'men, in all ages, have been so much imposed on by ridiculous stories of that kind') 'this very circumstance would be a full proof of a cheat'. (I think that Hume uses the phrase 'this very circumstance' to allude to the situation of our being offered a *ridiculous* story, ascribed to a new system of religion; and that he supposes that he somehow already knows that all such 'ridiculous stories' proffered hitherto have been false – which is why he speaks of a 'full proof' of a cheat, echoing his use in part 1 of the phrase 'a direct and full *proof*', in reference to the circumstance in which there is 'a uniform experience against' an alleged event of a certain kind.)

Given the purported unhappy track-record of religious miracle-reports (or, at least, of foundational ones), it is then supposed to be obvious that a new such report of a miracle is false, at least where the miracle is 'ascribed to' a 'new system of religion' (and, I surmise, even where it is ascribed to an old 'system of religion', as were the 'miracles . . . wrought in France upon the tomb of Abbé Paris'). The purported unhappy track-record of religious miracle-reports (or, at least, of foundational ones) is supposed to make 'the solution of the phenomenon' of a new such report 'obvious'. The purported unhappy track-record ('the violations of truth are more common in the testimony concerning religious miracles, than in that concerning any other matter of fact' – note the absence of a restriction to foundational religious miracles) is supposed to 'make us form a *general resolution*, never to *lend any attention* to' a new religious miracle-report (my emphases). In passages 31 and 38 Hume is not explaining why we should 'reject' (either refrain from believing, or believe to be false) a newly discovered religious miracle-report (or a foundational one, for a *new* 'system of religion'); *that* is supposed somehow to be already established. He is explaining why we should 'reject it without farther examination'; why we should not 'lend any attention to it, with whatever specious pretence it may be covered' (that is, *however good* the testimony may seem to be); why the solution of the phenomenon is 'obvious'; why we should *dismiss* it as being 'more properly a subject of derision than of argument.'

It cannot be the case that in passages 31 and 38 Hume means to be arguing for the basic point that we should 'reject' (either refrain from believing, or believe to be false) a religious miracle-report, foundational or otherwise. That point he must suppose to have been somehow already established. He cannot here be saying, about a newly presented religious miracle-report (foundational or otherwise): 'Look, it's a *religious* miracle-report. But see the *unhappy* track-record of religious miracle-reports ("the violations of truth are more common in the testimony concerning religious miracles, than in that concerning any other matter of fact"). So the report does not meet the requisite spiffy ("extremely high") standards. So don't believe it.' If Hume were here arguing in this Fogelinesque vein, the question would immediately arise: How do you *know* that the track-record of religious miracle-reports is so *unhappy*? How do you know that 'violations of truth are more common in the testimony concerning religious miracles, than in that concerning any other matter of fact'? And what would Hume imagine himself being able to say in response? Well, there are 'many instances of forged miracles [and the like] . . . in all ages'. How would he know that? Well, the forged miracles 'have either been detected by contrary evidence, or . . . detect themselves by their absurdity.' But, as passages 32–4 – *occurring right here*, in the middle of Hume's discussion of peculiarly *religious* miracle-reports – make plain, Hume clearly realizes (it is so obvious that he 'need not mention the difficulty') that it will scarcely ever be the case that the forged miracles are 'detected' by 'contrary evidence' available to historical inquiry ('the season is now past'; 'the records and witnesses, which might clear up the matter, have perished beyond recovery'). So the 'forged miracles' must mostly 'detect themselves by their absurdity'; *that* is how we know that 'violations of truth' are so very 'common in the testimony concerning religious miracles.' But what is this 'absurdity' which bespeaks the falsity of at least these historical religious miracle-reports? Well – and what else could Hume imagine himself to say? – it is their being *miracle*-reports, from *too few* witnesses; purported *violations of the most established laws of nature*, alleged on too slender evidence. ('And shall we, rather than have a recourse to so natural a solution, allow of a miraculous violation of the most established laws of nature?')

But why would a *miracle* propounded by what you say is not 'a sufficient number' of men be an 'absurdity'? Well, Hume must think that that point somehow has been established.

If Hume, in these passages, is arguing in the way which Fogelin avers, and it is simply 'an examination of historical records', rather than an application to history of 'philosophical grounds', which convinces Hume 'that testimony concerning religious miracles is notoriously unreliable', then his insertion of passages 32–4 *in the middle of this discussion* serves only to emphasize Hume's *inability to know*, simply through an examination of historical records, 'that testimony concerning religious miracles is notoriously unreliable'. This seems an implausible reading of Hume.

If, however, Hume is arguing here in the way I suggest, a way which presupposes that he has already established, chiefly on philosophical grounds, the 'many instances' of *forged* miracles and the like (they detect themselves 'by their absurdity'), and *goes on* to try to show that, given the thus-established especially unhappy track-record of religious miracle-reports, further religious miracle-reports should be dismissed without a hearing (rejected 'without farther examination'), then his insertion of passages 32–4 makes perfect sense. Hume is not here arguing for the *rejection* of a religious miracle-report, of that slender-evidenced sort which adorns the records of history, newly uncovered in a newspaper or a history book. (That were a point already made.) He is here arguing for its *peremptory* dismissal, for rejection 'without farther examination'. He is arguing that we should 'form a general resolution, never to lend *any attention* to it, with *whatever specious pretence* it may be covered' (my emphases). How apropos, then, that he notes the sceptical historian's peculiar difficulty in seeing through 'specious pretence'. Hume indeed reminds the skeptical historian of the true 'means of detection', the philosophical grounds which are 'always sufficient with the judicious and knowing'; why does he not simply advise the skeptical historian to apply these philosophical grounds to the new case of an uncovered religious miracle-report? In a way, of course, he does advise this (he calls our attention to the true 'means of detection'); but Hume knows that historians are not always philosophers, and that they have a natural professional tendency to, after all, start examining *historically* things better left unexamined historically. Hume thus wants the skeptical historian to form a general resolution against that which (quoting

Lord Bacon) 'depends in any degree upon religion'. Hume wants him to adopt henceforth an attitude of peremptory dismissal towards at least religious miracle-reports of the familiar kind. Hume wants to hear the laughter of 'just reasoners'. Now, an attitude of peremptory dismissal to religious miracle-reports is not obviously justified, save by way of an application of the 'philosophical grounds' *first* to the (*thereby*) known tragical (or comical) history of things religious.

This interpretation of what is going on in these passages is made all the stronger by what Hume says in 35 (which is the third of three passages which might have seemed to support Fogelin). Note, first, that at the *beginning* of the passage Hume takes it somehow to have been already established ('Upon the whole, then, it appears . . .') 'that no testimony for *any kind of* miracle has ever amounted to a probability' (my emphasis). How did Hume learn that none of those actual miracle-reports found in 'the records of history' ever amounted even to a probability ('much less to a proof')? He does not here appeal to the fact that these miracle-reports were *religious* miracle-reports, the issue of religion arising only *later* in this passage. Is it not manifest that Hume is here appealing to the supposed fact that 'there is not to be found, in all history, any miracle attested by a *sufficient number* of men' (of the right character and circumstance; my emphasis)? (In which case, Hume must think that he has established, philosophically, that there are [positive] numbers which are not 'a sufficient' number.) It seems obvious that, at least, Hume is here appealing to the (*just mentioned*, in 34) true 'means of detection', which are 'drawn from the very testimony itself of the reporters' and are 'always sufficient with the judicious and knowing.' What is drawn from the *very* testimony *itself* of the reporters cannot be any general, historically-gleaned knowledge of the especially unhappy track-record of religious miracle-reports. What is drawn from the very testimony itself of the reporters is, rather, that a *miracle* has been attested (*any kind of* miracle!) by *these few* witnesses; and this thing which is drawn from the testimony is 'always sufficient with the judicious and knowing', who know that *these few* witnesses are *too few* witnesses to a *miracle* (*any kind of* miracle!).

But perhaps what is 'drawn from the very testimony itself of the reporters' is that the testimony is to a *religious* miracle, and what the 'judicious and knowing' *know* is the especially unhappy track-record of religious miracle-reports, knowledge which comes not from philosophy

but from 'an examination of historical records'? (Or, it might be suggested, such purely historical knowledge, while not itself being 'drawn'
from the testimony, is – at least for the judicious and knowing – part
of that background knowledge which allows there to be any sort of
'drawing', of anything at all, from the testimony. After all, *some* background knowledge, at least concerning what the usual course of nature
is, is necessary for drawing 'from the very testimony itself' even the fact
that a *miracle* has been alleged. So why can't there be other background
historical knowledge?) And so, in some such way as this, Hume has
learned that 'no testimony for any kind of miracle has ever amounted to
a probability'?

But this cannot be what Hume means here. For, *first*, there would be
the question already discussed, of *how* the 'judicious and knowing'
learned, simply by studying history, of the especially unhappy track-
record of religious miracle-reports. Obviously not simply by studying
such historical records as Hume himself invokes, where in all cases but
one the 'detection' is philosophical *rather than* merely historical, by the
'absurdity' of the purported miracle *rather than* by historically accessible
'contrary evidence.' And, *second*, Hume has just gone out of his way (in
passages 32–4) to emphasize that such *historically*-gleaned knowledge
of the especially unhappy track-record of religious miracle-reports will
scarcely ever be possible. (Setting aside inductive scepticism – as of
course Hume himself does in this context – it is clear where the 'background knowledge' concerning 'the usual course of nature' is supposed
to come from: 'custom and experience'. And so there is no obvious
objection to an appeal to it in 'drawing from the testimony' the fact that
a miracle has been alleged. The objection, to a similar such appeal to a
purely historical knowledge of the especially unhappy track-record of
religious miracle-reports, is not that it could not, if we had it, be also
part of such background knowledge; but, rather, is that, on Hume's
own words, any such purely *historical* background knowledge seems
unattainable – 'the season is now past'; 'the records and witnesses,
which might clear up the matter, have perished beyond recovery'.) *Third*,
in the remarks at the beginning of this passage, Hume goes out of
his way to indicate that he is not speaking peculiarly about religious
miracles, but rather about 'any kind of miracle'. If it were Hume's
application of what are in general the only 'means of detection' which
'remain' which taught him that 'no testimony for any kind of miracle

has ever amounted to a probability', and Hume's application of these 'means of detection' invoked a premiss peculiarly about *religious* miracle-reports, Hume would not go out of his way to indicate that he is drawing a conclusion about *any kind of* miracle heretofore alleged. Even if (as a well-known remark in a letter of 1761 makes probable) Hume believes that all miracle-reports have been religious miracle-reports – he would not go out of his way to say 'any kind of miracle', making no appeal to its religious nature. *Fourth*, the very subject of *religious* miracle-reports arises only at the *end* of the passage, as being (obviously) a special circumstance, added to those general circumstances just invoked, concerning 'any kind of miracle'.

So the remarks about religion, at the end of 35, have nothing to do with the fact simply that hitherto available religious (or other) miracle-reports are to be *rejected*. That is a point somehow already settled. Thus the remarks serve some other purpose.

Finally, my interpretation of what Hume is doing in these passages which we are looking at, according to which he is *not* here arguing that we should 'reject' (either refrain from believing, or believe to be false) a newly uncovered religious miracle-report (of the familiar kind, lacking exotically strong testimonial evidence), *on the grounds* of our historically-ascertained knowledge of the especially unhappy track-record of such *religious* miracle-reports (Hume himself emphasizes our *inability* to acquire merely historically such knowledge, and, I say, the mere *rejection* of such a new religious miracle-report, of the familiar kind, is a point which in Hume's eyes is already settled, chiefly on philosophical grounds); but is, rather, arguing that we should form a *general resolution* 'never to lend any attention to' such a report, peremptorily dismissing it instead 'without farther examination', makes excellent sense, as Fogelin's interpretation does not, of the crucial final sentence of passage 35 (my emphases):

> But according to the principle here explained, this subtraction, with regard to all popular religions, amounts to *an entire annihilation*; and therefore we may *establish it as a maxim*, that no human testimony *can* have such force as to prove a miracle, and make it a just foundation for any such system of religion.

The 'principle here explained' is, I take it, the maxim from the end of part 1, now invoked as the claim that '[w]hen . . . these two kinds of experience [that assuring us of the general veracity of 'human testimony,' and that assuring us of 'the laws of nature'] are contrary [because there is human testimony to a *miracle*, to 'a miraculous violation of the most established laws of nature'], we have nothing to do but subtract the one from the other, and embrace an opinion, either on one side or the other, with that assurance which arises from the remainder.' Now, why, 'with regard to all popular religions' – with regard, I take it, to human testimony to a *religious* miracle – does this 'subtraction' amount to 'an entire annihilation'? Given the experience 'which gives authority to human testimony', why would testimony peculiarly to a religious miracle have its force *entirely* 'annihilated' by the force of that experience 'which assures us of the laws of nature,' so that – I take it – it is left having something like *no force* whatsoever? Its force *entirely disappears*, so that we are left with not even the *slightest* reason to suppose the religious miracle to have occurred? 'Outweighed', surely (for Hume); but why 'an entire annihilation'? Now, the Humean notions of 'subtraction' and 'annihilation' are rather opaque. However, it is difficult to understand this talk of the 'subtraction' as 'amounting to', in the case of a religious miracle, 'an entire annihilation,' as meaning anything other than *something* of the form: No human testimony 'can' ever prove the occurrence of a religious miracle. If something of that sort is what Hume means, then perhaps we can make sense of the 'therefore' when Hume goes on to say: 'and therefore we may establish it as a maxim, that no human testimony can have such force as to prove a miracle, and make it a just foundation for any ["such"] system of religion'. Assuming that the 'can' after the 'therefore' has the same sense (whatever it is exactly) as the 'can' in the suggested premiss, we would deem the argument to be valid, construed as an enthymeme:

(1') For anything x, for anything y, if y is a possible religious miracle and x is actual human testimony to the actual occurrence of y then it is not the case that x 'can' prove the actual occurrence of y.

(2') (For anything y, if y is a possible miracle then if y is a just foundation for a system of religion then y is a possible religious miracle.)

Therefore:

(3') For anything x, for anything y, if y is a possible miracle and x is actual human testimony to the actual occurrence of y then it is not the case that: x 'can' prove the actual occurrence of y and y is a just foundation for a system of religion.

(3') (on some reading of the 'can') is presumably what Hume's conclusion means: 'no human testimony [is something which] can ['have such force as to'] prove a miracle, and make it a just foundation for any ['such'] system of religion.' (So too, for the pithier restatement of the conclusion, at the beginning of passage 36: 'a miracle can never be proved, so as to be the foundation of a system of religion.')

It may be protested that Hume is claiming something stronger than this, something which (3') does not obviously imply. That is, it may be suggested that Hume's 'can' should be read in the stronger sense of implying that it is (absolutely) *impossible*: for a miracle to be proved (from human testimony, of course) and to be ('so as to be') the ('just') foundation of a system of religion. Now, Fogelin does not want to attribute this sort of impossibility claim to Hume, and I of course agree with him.[5] After his remarks about how 'for Hume, it is an empirical fact, amply illustrated by history, that testimony concerning religious miracles is notoriously unreliable', and how on 'the basis of this general fact about the quality of such testimony, the wise reasoner has ample grounds for rejecting it', Fogelin says:

> This does not mean that on a priori grounds no amount of testimony could ever establish the occurrence of a religious miracle. To alter Hume's own example, suppose that for eight days all was dark save for an illuminated face that simultaneously appeared throughout the world, speaking in a way intelligible to all, offering many proofs of his or her magnificence, and so on. (The story could be further filled in with universal cures, resurrections, whatever.) We would then have a case that does parallel Hume's example of a natural miracle, and it would surely be a matter of prejudice for him to reject the testimony in behalf of the religious miracle while accepting the testimony in behalf of the natural miracle. (29)

And, presumably, Fogelin would say that Hume will allow for the possibility of there being human testimony which establishes the occurrence of a religious miracle which then serves as a just foundation for a system of religion. (The First Church of the Illuminated Face.)

Fogelin and I agree about this. In short, when Hume says that 'no human testimony *can* have such force as to prove a miracle, and make it a just foundation for any . . . system of religion' (my emphasis, of course), he is not saying that this sort of thing is a sheer impossibility; rather, he is saying *something* along the lines of our (3'). So, too, with the premiss I've offered in Hume's behalf: that no human testimony 'can' ever prove the occurrence of a religious miracle; it is *something* along the lines of the possibility-friendly (1').

But what then is the force of 'can' in (1') and (3')? What is the force of 'can' in Hume's 'no human testimony can have such force as to . . .'? To say that no human testimony *can* do such-and-such – while, admittedly, not requiring an absolute impossibility of human testimony's doing such-and-such – is still *rather stronger* than simply saying that no human testimony ever *will* do such-and-such. The especially unhappy track-record of religious miracle-reports (supposing it existed) might perhaps justify a claim that 'a miracle *will* never be proved, so as to be the foundation of a system of religion'; but how would it justify Hume's claim that 'a miracle *can* never be proved, so as to be the foundation of a system of religion'?

It is a capital omission in Fogelin's discussion, that he simply ignores the fact that Hume says 'no human testimony *can*', rather than simply saying 'no human testimony *will*'. Without textual support, Fogelin weakens Hume's conclusion of part 2:

> . . . the task of part 2 is to show that reports of *religious* miracles have not in the past met these [allegedly 'appropriate', 'extremely high'] standards. Taking experience as his guide, Hume further concludes that there is no likelihood that they will ever do so. (9–10)

But, as we have just seen (in the very passage, 35, which Fogelin quotes (24) as containing Hume's 'ringing conclusion'), Hume does *not* simply conclude that *there is no likelihood that* human testimony *will ever* 'have such force as to prove a miracle, and make it a just foundation for any such system of religion'; Hume goes out of his way to say that 'we may establish it as a maxim' that no human testimony *can* do this! As is well-known to Hume scholars, in the original published version of this passage Hume had said at the beginning, not that 'no testimony for any kind of miracle has ever amounted to a probability', but that 'no testimony for any kind of miracle can ever possibly amount to a probability'; emending, in the 1768 edition, 'can ever possibly amount to' to 'has ever amounted to'. But Hume did *not* emend his final 'ringing conclusion': we still have 'no human testimony' *can*, not 'no human testimony' *will*. On Fogelin's construal of what is going on in the passage, this can only be viewed as an infelicity on Hume's part.

On my construal, Hume's decision not to emend the final sentence is easily explained, as being something other than an infelicity. Hume has already in mind here that *general resolution* which he wants us to form (mentioned explicitly in passage 38), 'never to lend any attention to' a further report of a *religious* miracle, 'with whatever specious pretence it may be covered'. Because 'the violations of truth are more common in the testimony concerning religious miracles, than in that concerning any other matter of fact', 'this must diminish very much [to the point of, as he earlier suggestively put it, 'an entire annihilation'] the authority of the former testimony'; we are 'never to lend any attention to it'; we are to 'reject it without farther examination'. Now, what is rejected 'without farther examination' can do very little. This is why, at the end of passage 35, he very deliberately says 'no human testimony can . . .' The 'can' is *normative*. Given the 'general resolution' which, as it were by law, deprives further *religious* miracle-reports of all power to persuade, and 'makes' at least 'all men of sense' not simply 'reject' such a report, 'but even reject it without farther examination', no human testimony *can* – properly, legitimately – henceforth 'have such force as to prove a miracle, and make it a just foundation for any such' *system of religion*; as Hume says, rather suggestively, 'we may establish it as a maxim'.

Observe what fine sense we are able to make of passage 35, when reading it in the context of the other passages we are looking at. For the reasons already explained, the passage, far from confirming Fogelin's interpretation of Hume, troubles it. But what troubles Fogelin's reading, troubles us not at all. At the beginning of the passage, Hume goes out of his way to assert, as a point already established, that 'no human testimony for *any kind of* miracle has ever amounted to a probability' (my emphasis); the circumstance of *religious* miracles is nowhere yet in sight. I say, as I have explained, that this obviously general point about miracle-reports hitherto available has (supposedly) already been established on historical *and philosophical* grounds.[6] When the issue of religious miracle-reports arises (later) in the passage, Hume speaks of 'an entire annihilation' of their evidential force, and suggests that 'therefore we may establish it as a maxim' that (rather strongly) 'no human testimony *can* have such force as to prove a miracle, and make it a just foundation for any such system of religion' (my emphasis). I have explained how the argument indicated by the 'therefore' may be construed. It is based chiefly on (1') above: For anything x, for anything y, if y is a possible religious miracle and x is actual human testimony to the actual occurrence of y then it is not the case that x 'can' prove the actual occurrence of y. The 'can' here, like that in the 'maxim' itself ((3') above), is normative. Adopting, because of the (supposedly) especially unhappy track-record of religious miracle-reports, the general resolution which Hume would have us, perforce, form ('make us form') – a resolute attitude of peremptory dismissal henceforth towards any religious miracle-report of the historically familiar kind; rejection 'without farther examination' – no human testimony, of that kind (exotic *possibilities* notwithstanding), 'can' henceforth, in the light of this resolution, prove the actual occurrence of a religious miracle (nor, a fortiori, of one which may serve as 'a just foundation for any . . . system of religion'). Hume would have us henceforth be *immune* to any faint temptation to be swayed by history's religion-confirming 'clouds of witnesses', or 'witnesses to these things', or brave men dying speaking the name of him whom they 'saw, and touched' again after an Easter morning. All this is 'specious pretence'. No more sea-partings, no more resurrections, no more healings, no more 'confirming signs and wonders', for the new, immune, Humean man, whose face is set against such things, with (as Lucian says) 'a mind as hard as diamond towards such matters . . . who, if he could not discover how it went, would at all events be convinced beforehand that though the method of the fraud escaped him, it was nevertheless all sham and could not possibly happen'.[7] I know many men who have made themselves immune to religion in just this Humean way.

So, what is going on in Hume's essay seems to be this. In the first part of the essay, Hume argues philosophically, just as has traditionally been supposed, for some claim at least as strong as the (H) from my book – roughly, for at least the claim that it is quite impossible for *solitary* human testimony to a miracle to render it credible. It was the main purpose of that book to show that there is no discernible good philosophical argument (Hume's own, or any other) even for that, rather minimal, Humean claim; nor, a fortiori, for anything stronger than it. Doubtless, Hume was intending to argue for something stronger; the testimony of 11 men, or of 500, he would claim also to be insufficient to establish the occurrence of a miracle. But Hume never tells us how big a number 'a sufficient number' of witnesses to a miracle would be. (Hence my choice to focus on his inability to establish even the most minimal version of the claim, rendering the obscure matter of 'how many' he would deem sufficient, otiose.) In the imaginary miracle of the eight days of darkness (passage 36), where there is a sky-filling torrent of human testimony (as opposed to a mere cloud), we seem to have 'a sufficient number' of witnesses (of the right kind, of course), whose testimony is 'very extensive and uniform'. That at least seems to be the chief reason why Hume says that this possible *miracle* (*he* calls it a 'miracle') would be 'of such a kind as to admit of proof from human testimony' ('though, perhaps, it will be impossible to find any such in all the records of history'). In the imaginary attestation to Queen Elizabeth's resurrection (passage 37), however, we seem *not* to have 'a sufficient number' of witnesses (of the right kind, of course) – though we rather obviously have *lots and lots* of witnesses of the right kind – to give Hume even 'the least inclination to believe so miraculous an event'. It would seem that the 'sufficient number' of witnesses (of the right kind, of course) is somewhere in between these two cases.

There is, of course, a further difference between the two cases, to which perhaps some attention should be given. The miracle of the eight days of *darkness* 'seems to have a tendency towards . . . catastrophe' ('[t]he decay, corruption, and dissolution of nature'), whereas the latter purported miracle is a *resurrection* (the very opposite of 'decay', I suppose) and (perhaps in part because of that?) 'so signal a violation of the laws of nature'. The gloomy first miracle chimes in with that 'decay, corruption, and dissolution of nature' which is 'rendered probable by so many analogies', and this seems to weigh with Hume in regard to whether that event 'comes within the reach of human testimony, if that testimony be very extensive and uniform'. Is Hume really suggesting that miracles involving 'decay' (such as, supposedly, eight days of darkness) have an easier evidential row to hoe than miracles involving some 'reversal' of decay, such as a resurrection? Perhaps, but let us charitably pass over the point. (It is because of entropy – the granddaddy of 'decay' – that the sun *shines*. Eight days of darkness, of the miraculous sort which Hume has in mind, would require an astonishing reversal of the natural 'decay' of the sun, far outstripping the reversal of 'decay' involved in a mere human resurrection.) In any event, whatever else may weigh with Hume as regard the acceptance of a miracle, we know that numbers weigh with him; else he would not have chided the records of history for failing to supply us with 'a sufficient number' of witnesses to the same miracle.

Thus armed with some supposedly-established philosophical criterion for the assessment of miracle-reports (at least as strong as my (H), but surely much stronger), Hume examines 'the records of history'. He finds no miracle-report, or collection of miracle-reports, for *any kind of* miracle, which satisfies the criterion. He thus concludes ('Upon the whole, then, it appears . . .') at the *beginning* of passage 35, 'that no testimony for any kind of miracle has ever amounted to a probability'. Hume's dismal assessment of the credibility of historically available miracle-reports has nothing to do with their being reports of *religious* miracles; it has to do with the philosophical lens through which Hume reads history, the supposedly-established philosophical criterion. As he emphasizes, the only 'means of detection' which 'remain', given that (as is obviously generally the case) 'the season is now past' for historical investigation ('the records and witnesses, which might clear up the matter, have perished beyond recovery'; except in the *unusual* case of Lucian), are those 'which must be drawn from the very testimony itself of the reporters.' What is drawn from that testimony (given our – in this context, uncontroversial – knowledge of the usual course of nature) is that a *miracle* is attested to by *these few* witnesses (however splendid the kind of witnesses). But this which is 'drawn from the very testimony itself of the reporters' is 'always sufficient with the judicious and knowing', because they (unlike 'the vulgar') know, the 'just reasoner' knows, the 'wise and learned' know – however inchoately – that these few witnesses to a miracle are too few. A miracle is a violation of the 'most established' laws of nature! The 'sufficient number' of witnesses (however splendid) necessary to override otherwise universal 'custom and experience', to override that 'infallible', that 'firm and unalterable experience' which 'has established these laws', must needs be (Hume, the philosopher, avers) very much greater than 'these few'.

This is the philosophical criterion which Hume appeals to in his *rejection* of the historically available miracle-reports. On his own words, there will scarcely ever be anything available to him, of a purely *historical* nature, which would suffice. It is only with the assistance of Lady Philosophy that Hume learns that there have been 'many instances' of 'forged miracles'.[8]

What, then, of reports of *religious* miracles? They are *already* to be 'rejected' (at least in the sense of not being believed), on the empirical and philosophical grounds we have been discussing; for Hume already (at the beginning of passage 35) purports to have found that no testimony for *any kind* of miracle has ever even 'amounted to a probability'. Their rejection has nothing to do with their being peculiarly reports of *religious* miracles. Hume evidently thinks that it has also already been established, on these same empirical and philosophical grounds, that (at least) many of these (religious) miracle-reports are to be 'rejected' in the stronger sense of being deemed false. (How else would Hume be in a position to claim to know that 'violations of truth' are so very 'common in the testimony concerning religious miracles'?) He then suggests (I suppose that 'suggests' would be the right word) that, because of this especially unhappy track-record of 'testimony concerning religious miracles' (a record thus already established on historical *and philosophical* grounds), we perforce somehow are led to form (it will 'make us form') 'a general resolution, never to lend any attention to' a religious miracle-report (at least, I surmise, of the historically familiar kind; mere exotic *possibilities* notwithstanding). (Would Hume 'lend any attention to' global reports about the 'illuminated face'? Let us suppose that he would.) And Hume thus supposes that, *in the light of this general resolution*, no human testimony *can* henceforth establish the occurrence of a *religious* miracle (at least of anything remotely like the historically familiar kind), and ('therefore', as we have seen) 'no human testimony can', henceforth, 'have such force as to prove a miracle, and make it a just foundation for any . . . system of religion'.

I have just now been describing the (general shape of) what seems to be Hume's reasoning in the essay; I am, of course, not endorsing that reasoning. The supposedly cogent 'philosophical grounds' which would establish even the very minimal (H) (or, a fortiori, anything stronger) are purely imaginary (as I have argued in detail in my book). Without these cogent 'philosophical grounds' the line of reasoning described above entirely collapses. There is nothing which shows us that 'no testimony for any kind of miracle has ever amounted to a probability, much less to a proof'. Without the supposed cogent philosophical grounds, there is nothing which establishes the alleged 'many instances' of 'forged miracles'. (A *purely historical* 'examination of historical records' is unavailing, as Hume himself takes pains to emphasize; the 'forged miracles' and the like must mostly detect *themselves* 'by their absurdity'.) There is thus nothing which establishes the existence of the alleged especially unhappy track-record of testimony concerning *religious* miracles. There is thus nothing at all which in any way obliges us to form the 'general resolution' of which Hume speaks, to adopt an attitude of peremptory dismissal ('without farther examination') towards religious miracle-reports (of the historically familiar kind, or otherwise). There is thus nothing which obliges us to 'establish it as a maxim' that no miracle 'can' ever be proved, so as to be the foundation of a system of religion. The world is thus made safe again for revealed religion.

Notes

1   David Johnson. *Hume, Holism, and Miracles* (Ithaca: Cornell University Press, 1999).
2   Robert J. Fogelin. *A Defense of Hume on Miracles* (Princeton: Princeton University Press, 2003), 3.
3   As for Fogelin's criticisms of me, they are incompetent. Attributing to Hume (as I do) the claim that *solitary* testimony is insufficient to establish a miracle, is obviously not attributing to him the claim that 'no testimony' is sufficient to establish a miracle; in the textually obvious sense of 'testimony' at issue in Hume, and indeed in Fogelin: individual *or collective* testimony; the testimony of one *or more* human beings. Fogelin has obviously misread, either me, or his stated definition of 'gross misreader'. (He is not far from irony.) Proper attention to my oft-repeated caveat undermines every criticism Fogelin makes of me. Did he ever notice the caveat? Well, in one of his quotations of me (37) he noticed it well enough to delete it by an ellipsis. On (the misquoted) page 18 of my book (as on both adjoining pages!), I was explicitly restricting my consideration to the case of solitary attestation. I thus left Hume free to say that a multiplicity of witnesses adds evidential force, beyond what comes simply from the observed reliability of the kind of witness, and that a vast number may trump in favour of the miracle. (This makes *perfect* sense, 'on Johnson's understanding of what Hume meant by a proof', given the caveat. And thus, Fogelin's complete failure to respond to the *textual evidence*, and the *argument*, I had given in favour of that understanding, becomes all the more noticeable.)
4   On page 10 of *Hume, Holism, and Miracles*, I had attributed the following, deliberately minimal, claim to Hume:
    (H) Where *m* is a possible event, allegedly actual and allegedly witnessed, and where *L* is (for us, now) an apparent law, which any actual occurrence of *m* would have violated, and where (thus) *L* is (for us, now) exceedingly well established, relative to a body of inductive evidence, as being a law of nature, then, at the very least, the testimony of *one* human witness (not identical to any of us) who claims to have observed *m*'s occurrence can never rightly convince us that *m* has occurred – the testimony of *one* such supposed witness to *m*'s

occurrence will always be 'outweighed' by the inductive evidence which so strongly supports *L*. Note the twice-occurring italicized '*one*'!

5 Before Fogelin (25), I had emphasized the importance of Hume's passage about the eight days of darkness, prefacing my quotation of it with the words: 'It is abundantly clear that Hume means to be using 'miracle' in *some* sense such that we neither know a priori that there are no miracles, nor even know a priori that there are no miracles rightly established by human testimony.' (*Hume, Holism, and Miracles*, 6.) Fogelin (32–3) chooses a peculiarly ungracious way of expressing his agreement with me that it is a 'mistake . . . to attribute to Hume an a priori argument against the possibility of a miracle or an a priori argument against the possibility that testimony can establish the occurrence of a miracle.'

(Suppose that Fogelin *now* says that the 'mistake' is to suppose that there is *any* kind of human testimony, such that Hume argues a priori that *that kind* of testimony cannot establish the occurrence of a miracle. Then he objects to himself. For he says that Hume argues that there is *a kind* of testimony – *testimony which does not meet 'extremely high' standards* – such that that kind of testimony *cannot* [remember Fogelin's 'must'] establish the occurrence of a miracle.)

6 I *of course* agree that there are *empirical, historical* grounds, as well as philosophical grounds, appealed to here. It has scarcely been suggested by me that for Hume the final evaluation of a miracle-report is based simply on the philosophical grounds from part 1 of Hume's essay. *Obviously*, before reaching a 'summary conclusion' about the status of a miracle, there is still at the very least *this* empirical matter to be addressed: count the number of witnesses. Fogelin seems not to have noticed this, in his curious remarks about what is, or is not, a 'self-contained argument.'

7 Lucian, 'Alexander the False Prophet', in the Loeb Classical Library's edition of Lucian's works, translated by A. M. Harmon, Volume IV (Cambridge, MA: Harvard University Press, 1925), 199. (I have changed Harmon's 'firm as adamant' to 'hard as diamond'.)

8 Hume has no chance of getting (even if he intended to; he never explicitly makes such an inference, nor does Fogelin suggest that he does, or should) from history to the 'many instances' of forged miracles, by way of anything about the 'contrariety' of religions. (But notice, in passage 24 of Hume's essay, the interesting word 'expressly', in Hume's phrase 'even for those which have not been expressly detected'.) Whatever Hume's intent, there is no reason to go along with his idea in passage 24 that 'all the prodigies of different ['contrary'] religions are to be regarded as contrary facts', or with his claim that each thus 'destroys the credit' of the others (so that, collectively, 'the testimony destroys itself'). Even *were* the facts 'contrary', there is no reason to suppose that the credit of the well-evidenced is 'destroyed' by the credit of that which is poorly evidenced; and some purported miracles may be preferentially well-evidenced. But there is also no reason to suppose that the facts are 'contrary', in the first place.

I don't believe that the Buddha flew in the sky (since the event is poorly evidenced), and I don't believe that Vespasian effected miraculous cures (since the cures, which are well-evidenced, are poorly evidenced as being miracles). But neither do I believe that such *miracles* did *not* occur. I simply abstain. For those who have already concluded that some miracles (preferentially and sufficiently well-evidenced as being miracles) occur, and that the best explanation of these occurrences involves a realm of intrusive supernatural agents, there is no barrier to a cautious abstention concerning the observable prodigies of other religions.

A Christian world is congenial collectively to those pagan miracles m_1, m_2, . . ., m_n, such that no m_1, m_2, . . ., m_k for $k \leq n$ collectively establish *with Bayesian certainty* anything incompatible with Christianity. To vary an analogy given in Jordan Howard Sobel's *Logic and Theism* (Cambridge: Cambridge University Press, 2004; n. 24, 596), 'suppose that a marble is to be drawn at random from an urn, of which there are two containing. Each contains marbles that are rough or smooth, and white and green': Urn A (1 rough and white, 999,998 smooth and white, 1 smooth and green), Urn B (999,999 rough and green, 1 smooth and white). Then, where A = 'The marble was drawn from Urn A' (which proposition is the analogue of Christianity), B = 'The marble was drawn from Urn B' (the analogue of the negation of Christianity), W = 'The marble drawn is white' (the analogue of the proposition asserting the occurrence of the Resurrection), R = 'The marble drawn is rough' (the analogue of the proposition asserting the occurrence of all the pagan miracles), although $\Pr(A/W) = \Pr(B/R) = .999999$, $\Pr(A/R \& W) = 1$ and $\Pr(B/R \& W) = 0$.

There is no principled path, simply from the contrariety of *religions*, to a discovery of 'many instances' of forged *miracles*.

CHAPTER 10

HUME AND THE PROBLEM OF EVIL

Michael Tooley

Introduction

The concept of evil

The problem of evil, in the sense relevant here, concerns the question of the reasonableness of believing in the existence of a deity with certain characteristics. In most discussions, the deity is God, understood as an omnipotent, omniscient and morally perfect person. But the problem of evil also arises, as Hume saw very clearly, for deities that are less than all-powerful, less than all-knowing and less than morally perfect.

What is the relevant concept of evil, in this context? Here it is useful to distinguish between axiological concepts and deontological ones. First, there are judgements about whether certain states of affairs make the world better or worse, whether those states are good or bad, desirable or undesirable. Such normative concepts – of good and bad, or desirable and undesirable, states of affairs – are axiological concepts.

Second, there are judgements about the rightness and wrongness of actions, about what one morally ought or ought not do, of what one's duty is, of whether a certain action violates someone's rights, and these concepts – of the rightness and wrongness of actions, of duties, of the rights of individuals, of what one should or should not do – are deontological concepts.

Given this distinction, should the problem of evil be understood axiologically or deontologically? Often, and I think most commonly in this context, evils are equated with states of affairs that, all things considered, are bad or undesirable: they are states of affairs that make the world a worse place. But one can also interpret the problem of evil in a deontological fashion, equating evils with states of affairs that a person should have prevented, if he could have done so.

Elsewhere (2008: 105–6), I have argued that the deontological interpretation is preferable. But for present purposes, either interpretation will be fine.

Evil and the reasonableness of belief in the existence of God

That many things in the world – tsunamis, earthquakes, the suffering of non-human animals and innocent children, human actions such as the carrying out of the Holocaust – certainly *appear* to be evil is not a controversial matter. But whether such things are really evils, all things considered, is disputed. Assume, however, that the world does continue genuine evils, and not merely apparent ones. How, then does the existence of such evils bear upon the reasonableness of belief in the existence of God?

First, the existence of evils can be used to show that certain arguments for the existence of God cannot establish that conclusion, or even render it probable. For some arguments, of course, one need not appeal to evil to make that point. If someone argues for the existence of a first cause, or an unmoved mover, or a necessary being having its necessity of itself, and then claims that this is what everyone understands by the term 'God', one can point out that no reason has been offered for thinking that the entity in question is even a person, let alone omnipotent, omniscient and perfectly good. By contrast, with the type of argument that Hume was concerned with when he discussed the problem of evil – namely, arguments from the existence of order in the world to the existence of a designer, or intelligent cause of that order – one does have a type of argument that, if sound, shows that there is a person who, even if not omnipotent and omniscient, is at least extremely powerful and very knowledgeable. But such arguments do not support conclusions about the moral character of such a person, and so it is at this point that the existence of evils becomes crucial. For in providing a reason for holding that the one is not justified in attributing even moral goodness to such a being, let alone moral perfection, it supports the conclusion that that argument in question cannot be a successful argument for the existence of *God*.

The existence of evils, then, can serve to block arguments for the existence of God. But a second, and very familiar possibility, is that the existence of evils can also provide the basis of arguments against the existence of God.

A very important distinction here is between deductive, or logical incompatibility, versions of the argument from evil, and inductive, or evidential, or probabilistic versions of the argument. According to the former, there are facts about the existence of evils in the world that are logically incompatible with the existence of God. Thus, some have held that the mere existence of any evil whatsoever is incompatible with the existence of God; others, that that certain types of evil – such as natural evils – are incompatible with the existence of God; and others, that it is the amount of evil in the world, or the fact that some people suffer horrendous evils, that logically precludes the existence of God.

Inductive (or evidential, or probabilistic) versions of the argument from evil, by contrast, do not claim that there are facts about the evils in the world that are logically incompatible with the existence of God. The claim is rather that there are facts about the evils found in the world that render the existence of God at the very least unlikely, and perhaps extremely so.

Hume's use of the existence of evils

The preceding discussion suggests two very different ways in which Hume might be employing the existence of evils. First, he might be appealing to the existence of evils simply to undercut certain arguments for the existence of God. In particular, he might be appealing to evils to show that, whatever the merits of the argument from order to design may be, it can neither establish, nor render probable, the existence of a morally good deity.

Second, Hume might be advancing a version of the argument from evil, and that in turn could take the form either of an argument that claims that facts about evil are logically incompatible with the existence of God, or of an argument that claims, more modestly, that the apparent evils found in the world render the existence of God unlikely.

Hume and the existence of a dity

Before turning to Hume's discussion of evil, and its bearing upon the existence of God, it is worth considering what Hume's views were on the existence of a deity. This question is not without difficulty, but I think that J. C. A. Gaskin, in his very impressive and dispassionate book, *Hume's Philosophy of Religion* (1978), set out and defended a clear and very plausible answer to that question. Before considering Gaskin's answer, however, let us ask what the source of the difficulty here is. The answer is that there are at least three sources, two connected with Hume's *Dialogues Concerning Natural Religion*, and the other with Hume's other major writing on religion, his *Natural History of Religion*. First of all, then, as regard the *Dialogues*, three very different views concerning the existence of a deity are defended by the three parti- cipants in the *Dialogue* – Demea, Cleanthes and Philo – and there has not been unanimous agreement among Hume scholars as to which person speaks for Hume. On this matter, however, it seems to me that Norman Kemp Smith, in his long introduction to Hume's *Dialogues Concerning Natural Religion* (1935, 58–75 and 97–123), offered both very strong positive support for the view that it was Philo who consistently expressed Hume's own views, and also very detailed and convincing criticisms of scholars who had defended a different view. Still, Kemp Smith's view did not go unchallenged, with James Noxon (1964), in particular, advancing objections. But these and other attempts to undermine Kemp Smith's interpretations are discussed at length by Gaskin (1978, 159–66), where he both answers Noxon's points in detail, and offers further support for Kemp Smith's view. It seems to me, then, that the case for the claim that it is Philo who speaks for Hume is very strong.

The second source of the difficulty concerns the question as to precisely what Philo's view is in the *Dialogues*. On the one hand, in Parts I though XI, Philo sets out and vigorously defends several objections to arguments from order in the world to an intelligent source of that order. On the other hand, at the very beginning of Part XII, we find Philo saying, 'A purpose, an intention, a design strikes everywhere the most careless, the most stupid thinker; and no man can be so hardened in absurd systems as at all times to reject it.' (1980: 77). He then immedi- ately adds, '. . . and thus all the sciences almost lead us insensibly to acknowledge a first intelligent Author; and their authority is often so much the greater, as they do not directly express that intention'. (78)

Following immediately upon the highly critical discussion of the argument from order to design that has preceded, this is rather jarring. But before considering this second difficulty, let us turn to the third, and closely related one. It arises out of an apparent conflict between what Hume's discussion in the *Dialogues*, and what he says in his *Natural History of Religion*. Thus, in the former, Hume subjects the argument from order to design to an intense and sustained critical scrutiny, directing many objections of various kinds against that argument, and many philosophers have viewed Hume as having shown that the argument is unsound. But in the *Natural History of Religion*, the reader is confronted, at the very beginning, with the following passage:

> As every enquiry, which regards religion, is of the utmost importance, there are two questions in particular, which challenge our attention, to wit, that concerning its foundation in reason, and that concerning its origin in human nature. Happily the first question, which is the most important, admits of the most obvious, at least, the clearest solution. The whole frame of nature bespeaks an intelligent author; and no rational enquirer can, after serious reflection, suspend his belief a moment with regard to the primary principles of genuine Theism and Religion. (1993: 134)

Moreover, similar remarks are found elsewhere in the *Natural History of Religion*. Thus, a bit later, after referring to the idea of a 'perfect Being, who bestowed order on the whole frame of nature', Hume says, concerning the possibility of an argument in support of the existence of such a being, 'I allow that the order and frame of the universe, when accurately examined, afford such an argument . . .' (1993: 136).

Or again, when discussing the beliefs of ordinary people, Hume says:

> While they confine themselves to the notion of a perfect being, the creator of the world, they coincide, by chance, with the principles of reason and true philosophy; though they are guided to that notion, not by reason, of which they are in a great measure incapable, but by the adulation and fears of the most vulgar superstition. (1993: 155)

What is one to make of this? The correct answer, it seems to me, is that defended at length and very forcefully by J. C. A. Gaskin, in *Hume's Philosophy of Religion*. As Gaskin argues there, Hume accepts what Gaskin refers to as 'attenuated deism' (168). Thus, on the one hand, Hume does hold – the extended attempts, in the *Dialogues*, to blunt the force of an argument from order to design notwithstanding – that the most likely view is that the order in the world had an intelligent cause. But Hume also holds that such an argument does not show that such an intelligent cause has the attributes – especially that of moral perfection – possessed by the God of monotheism.

Consider, in the light of this view, the famous remarks by the character Pamphilus at the very beginning of the *Dialogues*:

> What truth so obvious, so certain, as the *being* of a God, which the most ignorant ages have acknowledged, for which he most refined geniuses have ambitiously striven to provide new proofs and arguments? Which truth so important as this, which is the ground of all our hopes, the surest foundation of morality, the firmest support of society, and the only principle which ought never to be a moment absent from our thoughts and meditations? But, in treating of this obvious and important truth, what obscure questions occur concerning the *nature* of that Divine Being; his attributes, his decrees, his plan of providence? (1980: 2)

Now Pamphilus here clearly does not in general speak for Hume, for he advances a number of views that Hume rejects and argues against – such as the claim that morality is to founded on the existence of a deity. But in having Pamphilus introduces the distinction between the question of the existence of a deity, and the question of the nature of such a being, Hume emphasizes the words '*being*' and '*nature*', and the reason, surely, is that Hume is indicating that the distinction between the question of the existence of an intelligent source of order in the world, and the further question of the properties of such a being, is crucial for the what follows in the *Dialogues*.

Consider, finally, the summing up that Philo offers at the beginning of the penultimate paragraph of the *Dialogues* – a paragraph that, as Gaskin points out (1980: 129, fn 1), was added in Hume's final revision of his manuscript before his death in 1776:

> If the whole of natural theology, as some people seem to maintain, resolves itself into one simple, though somewhat ambiguous, at least undefined proposition, *That the cause or causes of order in the universe probably bear some remote analogy to human intelligence*: If this proposition be not capable of extension, variation, or more particular explication: If it affords no inference that affects

human life, or can be the source of any action or forbearance: And if the analogy, imperfect as it is, can be carried no further than to the human intelligence, and cannot be transferred, with any appearance of probability, to the other qualities of the mind: If this really be the case, what can the most inquisitive, contemplative, and religious man do more than give a plain, philosophical assent to the proposition, as often as it occurs; and believe that the arguments on which it is established exceed the objections which lie against it? (1980: 88)

This passage is a clear and very forceful statement of an 'attenuated deism' –indeed, a highly attenuated deism. Coming at the very end of the *Dialogues*, in a speech by Philo, and one added by Hume in his final revision, surely there is excellent reason for thinking that it expresses Hume's own view, especially given its coherence with Hume's statements about the argument from order in his *Natural History of Religion*.

Are there any reasons for doubting this conclusion? Hume was, of course, often scathing in his comments upon historical religions, especially Christianity. But his objections to such 'revealed' religions centre upon features that are not present in a 'plain, philosophical assent' to the proposition he mentions as possibly summing up 'the whole of natural theology'.

Still, one might think it surprising, given Hume's skeptical bent of mind, and his extremely impressive critical faculties, that he would accept even such a highly attenuated and strongly circumscribed proposition. But if one considers how things were before the publication by Charles Darwin of *The Origin of Species* in 1859, I think that Hume's acceptance of the proposition in question ceases to be puzzling. For the existence of complex ordered structures such as one finds in living things is surely *a priori* very improbable, and so really calls for explanation, and while the idea of an evolutionary explanation was one that Hume considered, until its detailed development by Darwin, and his amassing of evidence in support of it, such a hypothesis could not, I think, plausibly be viewed as a serious competitor to the idea of an intelligent source of the order in the world.

Hume on evil

Philo, speaking for Hume, insists that one cannot move, with any appearance of probability, beyond the bare and highly qualified proposition that '*the cause or causes of order in the universe probably bear some remote analogy to human intelligence*' to *any* further conclusion about the attributes of such a cause or causes. But Hume was especially concerned with extensions involving any 'inference that affects human life'. What would be crucial in that regard, however, would be a conclusion concerning the moral goodness of the cause (or causes) of order. For if an intelligent being is responsible for the order in the universe, but that being, rather than being morally good, let alone morally perfect, is either morally indifferent to good and evil, or else morally evil itself, the existence of such a being is unlikely to make any difference with regard to how humans ought to live.

For this reason, the existence of evil is crucial for Hume's attenuated deism, since it is precisely the existence of evil that blocks, if Hume is right, any extension that would support a conclusion that affects human life.

Hume's discussion in Part X of the dialogues

The appeal to concrete cases of evil

Hume's initial focus, then, is on blocking a certain inference – namely, from the proposition that there probably is an intelligent source of order in the world to the conclusion that that being is morally good. He begins, in Part X, then, with a detailed description of highly undesirable things found in the world, starting out with the suffering that animals inflict upon other animals – 'And thus on each hand, before and behind, above and below, every animal is surrounded with enemies, which incessantly seek his misery and destruction' (1980: 96), and then moving on to the evils that humans suffer, starting with those they inflict upon each other:

> Man is the greatest enemy of man. Oppression, injustice, contempt, contumely, violence, sedition, war, calumny, treachery, fraud; by these they mutually torment each other, and they would soon dissolve that society which they had formed were it not for the dread of still greater ills which must attend their separation. (1980: 60)

Hume then refers to terrible diseases that affect human life:

> But though these external insults, said *Demea*, from animals, from men, from all the elements, which assault us, form a frightful catalogue of woes, they are

nothing in comparison of those which arise within ourselves, from the distempered condition of our mind and body. How many lie under the lingering torment of diseases? Hear the pathetic enumeration of the great poet.

> Intestine stone and ulcer, colic – pangs,
> Demoniac frenzy, moping melancholy,
> And moon – struck madness, pining atrophy,
> Marasmus, and wide – wasting pestilence.
> Dire was the tossing, deep the groans: *Despair*
> Tended the sick, busiest from couch to couch.
> And over them triumphant *Death* his dart
> Shook: but delay'd to strike, though oft invok'd
> With vows, as their chief good and final hope.[1]
> (1980: 60–1)

This focus of Hume upon concrete cases of evil is very important. For much of the twentieth century, philosophers focused almost entirely on abstract formulations of the argument from evil. Moreover, those discussions usually centred on incompatibility versions of the argument, so the questions debated were generally whether the existence of any evil whatsoever is, or is not, incompatible with the existence of God, or whether the existence of certain types of evil – such as natural evil – or the existence of a certain amount of evil, is or is not incompatible with the existence of God. Occasionally, evidential or probabilistic versions of the argument from evil were considered, but such discussions – including the lengthy one by Alvin Plantinga in his 1979 article 'The Probabilistic Argument from Evil' – again failed to focus on concrete cases of evils.

As I have argued elsewhere (2008: 101–5), this failure to focus on concrete cases of evil was a serious mistake. A turning point came, however, in 1979, with William Rowe's article, 'The Problem of Evil and Some Varieties of Atheism'. Rowe, in contrast to the type of discussion that had dominated the philosophical landscape for many years, offered a concrete formulation of the argument from evil, focusing upon the agonizing death of an animal in a forest fire. Because of this article, there was a gradual shift from abstract formulations of the argument from evil to much more concrete formulations.

Hume, then, by reminding the reader of the multitude of terrible forms that suffering takes was approaching the problem of evil in exactly the right way.

An incompatibility version of the argument from evil

With vivid cases of evils before us, Philo then offers a statement of the argument from evil:

> And is it possible, *Cleanthes,* said *Philo,* that after all these reflections, and infinitely more which might be suggested, you can still persevere in your anthropomorphism, and assert the moral attributes of the Deity, his justice, benevolence, mercy, and rectitude, to be of the same nature with these virtues in human creatures? His power, we allow, is infinite; whatever he wills is executed: But neither man nor any other animal is happy; therefore, he does not will their happiness. His wisdom is infinite; He is never mistaken in choosing the means to any end; But the course of nature tends not to human or animal felicity: Therefore, it is not established for that purpose. Through the whole compass of human knowledge there are no inferences more certain and infallible than these. In what respect, then, do his benevolence and mercy resemble the benevolence and mercy of men?
>   Epicurus' old questions are yet unanswered.
>   Is he willing to prevent evil, but not able? then is he impotent. Is he able, but not willing? then is he malevolent. Is he both able and willing? whence then is evil? (1980: 63)

How are we to understand this argument? Is Hume advancing an incompatibility version of the argument? That is certainly the view advanced by Nelson Pike in his well-known discussion, 'Hume on Evil' (1963: 182):

> Moving now to the details of the matter, we may, I think, formulate Philo's first challenge to Cleanthes as follows:
>
> (1) The world contains instances of suffering.
> (2) God exists and is omnipotent and omniscient.
> (3) God exists and is perfectly good.
>
> According to the view advanced by Philo, these three statements constitute an 'inconsistent triad' (66)
>
> Given the words 'inconsistent triad', there can surely be no doubt about what Hume, in the person of Philo, must be claiming.

But those words are nowhere to be found on page 66 of the edition of the *Dialogues*, edited by David Aiken (1959) from which Pike is quoting. Indeed, neither word is found anywhere in either Part X or Part XI.

How do things stand once one sets aside Pike's hallucination of the words 'inconsistent triad'? Like Pike, I certainly think that Philo is here claiming that the existence of evil is logically incompatible with the existence of an omnipotent, omniscient and perfectly good person. For Philo claims that if someone is able to prevent evil, and fails to do so, then that person is malevolent.

Now if 'evil' means something that ought, *all things considered*, to be prevented, then any being who knows of such an evil, and fails to prevent it, is certainly malevolent. But Hume, at this point, is over-looking the possibility that what certainly *appear* to be evils, all things considered, may not be so. In particular, Hume fails to consider either of the following two, apparent possibilities.

First of all, it may be that what are evils, considered in themselves, are logically necessary for greater goods. More explicitly, perhaps there can be states of affairs S and T where state of affairs T is intrinsically bad, but where the existence of T is logically necessary for the existence of S, and where the combination of S and T is morally better than the absence of both. Thus, for example, some theists have held that a world where people respond compassionately to the sufferings of others is better than a world that lacks both the suffering and the compassionate responses.

Second, perhaps there is such a thing as libertarian free will, and, if so, perhaps, a world containing libertarian free will, along with the possibility of immoral actions, is a better world than one that does not contain libertarian free will.

One problem with the second of these is that even if one grants, for the sake of argument, both that one can make sense of the idea of libertarian free will, and also that libertarian free will may be so valuable that it is morally permissible to create a world with libertarian free will, thereby running the risk that people will commit morally wrong actions, this still leaves one with the problem of why various *morally horrendous* actions have not been not prevented if there is a being capable of doing so.

The first response is also very weak, *if* the suggestion is that if one reflects closely upon the evils in the world, one can see that they are logically necessary for greater goods. For what are the greater goods for which earthquakes and tsunamis killing hundreds of thousand innocent people, including children, are logically necessary?

The suggestion, however, can instead be that, while there are no goods that we are aware of for which various evils are logically necessary, there may be relevant goods that lie outside the scope of human knowledge, and then an argument is needed to show that this is unlikely. But then one has shifted – as one should do – from an incompatibility version of the argument from evil to an evidential or probabilistic one.

The relative amounts of good versus evil

Philo next considers the relative amounts of pleasure and pain in the world (1980: 63–6). This is a line of thought that appears to go back a long way in Hume, for in 1993, a part of a manuscript came to light in which Hume set out an argument based upon this sort of comparison, and M. A. Stewart, in his article 'An early fragment on evil', has argued very plausibly, I think, that 'a significant part of Hume's mature philosophy of religion was fully worked out by around the time of the *Treatise* . . .' (1993: 165).

In that fragment, Hume considers an argument based upon comparing the amount of goodness or happiness in the universe with the amount of evil or misery (Stewart, 1993: 166):

> Whether the Author of Nature be benevolent or not can only be prov'd by the Effects, & by the Predominancy either of Good or Evil, of Happiness or Misery, in the Universe. If the Good prevail much above Evil, we may, perhaps, presume, that the Author of the Universe, if intelligent, is also a benevolent Principle. If Evil prevail much above Good, we may draw a contrary inference.

Hume says that arriving at a confident view concerning which predominates is not easy since, on the one hand, there are very intense pains, often of great duration, but, on the other hand, there are much more frequent pleasures, albeit almost always much less intense, and much more transitory. But Hume argues that, this difficulty notwithstanding, one can still arrive at an important conclusion (Stewart, 1993: 168):

> But tho' it be difficult to decide this Question, whether there be more Good than Evil in the Universe, we may, perhaps, find Means, independent of it, to decide, in some tolerable manner, that other Question concerning the Benevolence of the Deity. Were Evil predominant in the World, there wou'd evidently remain no Proofs of Benevolence in the supreme Being. But even if Good be predominant; since it prevails in so small a Degree, and is counter ballanc'd by so many Ills; it can never afford any Proof of that Attribute. Pains & Pleasures seem to be scatter'd

indifferently thro Life, as Heat & Cold, Moist & Dry are disperst thro the Universe; & if the one prevails a little above the other, this is what will naturally happen in any Mixture of Principles, where an exact Equality is not expressly intended. On every Occasion, Nature seems to employ either.

In the related discussion in the *Dialogues*, Philo advances three main contentions. First, he argues that it cannot be shown that human happiness in this world outbalances human misery. Second, he then defends, again, a logical incompatibility version of the argument from evil:

But allowing you what never will be believed, at least, what you never possibly can prove, that animal or, at least, human happiness in this life exceeds its misery, you have yet done nothing; for this is not, by any means, what we expect from infinite power, infinite wisdom, and infinite goodness. Why is there any misery at all in the world? Not by chance, surely. From some cause then. Is it from the intention of the Deity? But he is perfectly benevolent. Is it contrary to his intention? But he is almighty. Nothing can shake the solidity of this reasoning, so short, so clear, so decisive, except we assert that these subjects exceed all human capacity, and that our common measures of truth and falsehood are not applicable to them; a topic which I have all along insisted on, but which you have, from the beginning, rejected with scorn and indignation. (1980: 65–6)

Finally, Philo argues that even if he is mistaken on this matter, the distribution of good and evil in the world undercuts any attempt to demonstrate the existence of a perfectly good deity:

But I will be contented to retire still from this retrenchment, for I deny that you can ever force me in it. I will allow that pain or misery in man is *compatible* with infinite power and goodness in the Deity, even in your sense of these attributes: what are you advanced by all these concessions? A mere possible compatibility is not sufficient. You must *prove* these pure, unmixed and uncontrollable attributes from the present mixed and confused phenomena, and from these alone. A hopeful undertaking! Were the phenomena ever so pure and unmixed, yet, being finite, they would be insufficient for that purpose. How much more, where they are also so jarring and discordant! (1980: 66)

At this point, then, it seems that Hume's focus is upon the idea that the inference cannot possibly succeed. The question, accordingly, is whether Hume will, at any point, claim that an inference to a *contrary conclusion* is justified – that is, whether he will advance an inductive version of the argument from evil.

Hume's discussion – Part XI

The shift to a finite deity

At the beginning of this part, Cleanthes makes the important move of shifting from an infinite God, a god who is omnipotent, omniscient and perfectly good, to one who is great in these respects, but finite. His reason for doing so is as follows:

> But supposing the Author of Nature to be finitely perfect, though far exceeding mankind, a satisfactory account may then be given of natural and moral evil, and every untoward phenomenon be explained and adjusted. A lesser evil may then be chosen in order to avoid a greater; inconveniences be submitted to in order to reach a desirable end; and, in a word, benevolence, regulated by wisdom and limited by necessity, may produce just such a world as the present. (1980: 67)

Philo's immediate response to this shift to a finite deity is then as follows (1980: 105–6):

> My sentiments, replied *Philo,* are not worth being made a mystery of; and, therefore, without any ceremony, I shall deliver what occurs to me with regard to the present subject. It must, I think, be allowed that, if a very limited intelligence whom we shall suppose utterly unacquainted with the universe were assured that it were the production of a very good, wise, and powerful being, however finite, he would, from his conjectures, form *beforehand* a different notion of it from what we find it to be by experience; nor would he ever imagine, merely from these attributes of the cause of which he is informed, that the effect could be so full of vice and misery and disorder, as it appears in this life. Supposing now that this person were brought into the world, still assured that it was the workmanship of such a sublime and benevolent being, he might, perhaps, be surprised at the disappointment, but would never retract his former belief if founded on any very solid argument; since such a limited intelligence must be sensible of his own blindness and ignorance, and must allow that there may be many solutions of those phenomena which will forever escape his comprehension. But supposing, which is the real case with regard to man, that this creature is not antecedently convinced of a supreme intelligence, benevolent, and powerful, but is left to gather such a belief from the appearances of things; this entirely alters the case, nor will he ever find any reason for such a conclusion. (1980: 67–8)

Philo's advances two main claims here. First, if someone, knowing nothing about the world, or, at least, nothing about the distribution of good and evil in it, were told that it was 'the production of a very good, wise, and powerful being, however finite', he would be surprised when he saw what the world was like.

Second, if one had previously formed, on the basis of 'any very solid argument', the belief that the world was 'the production of a very good, wise, and powerful being, however finite', there would be no need for him to retract that opinion on seeing what the world was like.

The reasonableness of the second claim is very much open to question. I would argue that it would need to be an *extremely* solid argument indeed, since, short of the ontological argument, I think it is not at all easy to see what argument could suffice.

An inference to be avoided

As regard the first claim, the question is whether Hume is here embracing the following argument:

The Simple Argument from Surprise to Improbability

Let p = The world was produced by a very good, wise, and powerful being.
  q = The world does not have a very satisfactory balance of good over evil.

(1) Given p, q is surprising.
(2) If q is surprising given p, then the probability of q given p is low.
Therefore:

(3) The probability of q given p is low.
(4) For any propositions r and s, if probability of s given r is low, then probability of r given s is low.
Therefore:

(5) The probability of p given q is low.

That is, the probability that the world was produced by a very good, wise and powerful being is low given that the world does not have a very satisfactory balance of good over evil.

Now Hume does not, in the passage quoted, or anywhere else, advance this argument. His idea is simply that the fact that the relative amounts of goodness and evil in the world would be surprising if the world were produced by a very good, wise and powerful being *serves to block* a certain inference:

In short, I repeat the question: Is the world, considered in general and as it appears to us in this life, different from what a man or such a limited being would, *before-hand*, expect from a very powerful, wise, and benevolent Deity? It must be strange prejudice to assert the contrary. And from thence I conclude that, however consistent the world may be, allowing certain suppositions and conjectures with the idea of such a Deity, it can never afford us an inference concerning his existence. The consistency is not absolutely denied, only the inference. Conjectures, especially where infinity is excluded from the divine attributes, may perhaps be sufficient to prove a consistency, but can never be foundations for any inference. (1980: 69)

But now the question is *how* the fact that the relative amounts of goodness and evil in the world would be surprising if the world were the production of a very good, wise and powerful being can serve to block the inference in question, and it would seem that it can do so only if the relative amounts of goodness and evil in the world makes it more likely than not that the world is not the production of a very good, wise and powerful being. So must not Hume be *implicitly* making an inference of the following logical form: The probability of *q* given *p* is low; therefore, the probability of *p* given *q* is low?

Why would that be problematic? The answer is that although that type of inference may seem plausible, it is not in general inductively sound. For consider the following propositions:

r = John weighs between 150 pounds and 200 pounds.
s = John weighs between 164 pounds and 165 pounds.

The probability of *s* given *r* is quite low, but the probability of *r* given *s*, rather than being low, is equal to one, since *s* entails *r*.

Or consider:

t = A very powerful supernatural being wanted Joshua to win the battle.
u = The sun stood still during the battle, which enabled Joshua to win.

Even given *t*, *u* would still be relatively surprising, since the very powerful supernatural being might have chosen not to intervene, or might have been prevented by a different powerful supernatural being, or might have intervened, but in any number of other, much less dramatic ways. So the probability of *u* given *t* seems rather low. But the probability of *t* given *u*, on the other hand, seems reasonably high.

An Alternative Line of Argument
Hume may have succumbed, then, to a tempting but unsound inference. But, as I shall now argue, that need not have been the case.

A Slightly More Complex Argument from Surprise to Improbability.

Let W be a proposition that describes the totality of good and evil in our world, and suppose one thought the following two hypotheses were *a priori* equally likely:

G: The cause or causes of the world are good.
I: The cause or causes of the world are indifferent to good and evil.[2]

Then one would have:

(1) $Pr(G) = Pr(I)$

Suppose, further, one thought that W would be surprising given G, but not given I. Then the probability of W given G would be less than the probability of W given I, so one would have:

(2) $Pr(W/G) < Pr(W/I)$

But the following are analytically true by virtue of the definition of conditional probability:

(3) $Pr(I/W) \times Pr(W) = Pr(W \& I) = Pr(W/I) \times Pr(I)$

(4) $Pr(G/W) \times Pr(W) = Pr(W \& G) = Pr(W/G) \times Pr(G)$

Dividing equation (3) by equation (4) gives one:

(5) $\dfrac{Pr(I/W)}{Pr(G/W)} \times \dfrac{Pr(W)}{Pr(W)} = \dfrac{Pr(W \& I)}{Pr(W \& G)} = \dfrac{Pr(W/I)}{Pr(W/G)} \times \dfrac{Pr(I)}{Pr(G)}$

Dropping out the $\dfrac{Pr(W \& I)}{Pr(W \& G)}$ term, and using (1) gives one:

(6) $\dfrac{Pr(I/W)}{Pr(G/W)} = \dfrac{Pr(W \& I)}{Pr(W \& G)}$

In view of (2), $\dfrac{Pr(W/I)}{Pr(W/G)} > 1$.

Hence we have:

(7) $Pr(I/W) > Pr(G/W)$

The conclusion, accordingly, is that if it is just as likely that the cause or causes of the world are indifferent to good and evil as that they are good, and if the situation as regard good and evil in the world is more surprising, and therefore less probable, on the assumption that the cause or causes of the world are good than on the assumption that they are indifferent to good and evil, then it follows that the first of these hypotheses is less likely than the second. But one can also draw a further conclusion, given the following, analytically true proposition:

(8) $I \Rightarrow$ Not G

That is, if I is true, then, necessarily, G is false.

But given that this is so, the probability that G is false must be at least as great as the probability that I is true. So we have:

(9) $\Pr(\text{Not } G/W) \geq \Pr(I/W)$

This together with (7) then entails:

(10) $\Pr(\text{Not } G/W) \geq \Pr(G/W)$

So the probability that God does not exist, given information W concerning the good and bad states of affairs to be found in the world, is greater than the probability that God does exist, given information W.

Once again, this is not an argument that Hume is advancing at this stage. My point, however, is that given the claim that Hume does advance – namely, that the relative amounts of goodness and evil are surprising, given the hypothesis that the cause or causes of the world are good – all that needs to be added to produce a valid argument for the conclusion that the probability of its being false that that the cause or causes of the world are good is higher than the probability of its being true are the following two claims, both of which certainly seem to be ones that Hume would accept:

a   the relative amounts of goodness and evil found in the world are not surprising, given the hypothesis that the cause or causes of the world are indifferent to good and evil,

and

b   the hypothesis that the cause or causes of the world are indifferent to good and evil is no less likely, *a priori*, than the hypothesis that the cause or causes of the world are good.

In view of these connections, may it not have been the case that Hume sensed that the proposition that the relative amounts of goodness and evil are surprising, given the hypothesis that the cause or causes of the world are good, had an evidential bearing upon the hypothesis that the cause or causes of the world are good, but lacked the probability framework that would have enabled him to show that that intuition is correct?

Four Very General Sources of Evil

Next, Philo describes '*four* circumstances on which depend all or the greatest part of the ills that molest sensible creatures . . .' With regard to these, he says that 'it is not impossible but all these circumstances may be necessary and unavoidable'. But he also says, 'None of them appear to human reason in the least degree necessary or unavoidable, nor can we suppose them such, without the utmost license of imagination' (1980: 69).

But if this is right, does not this mean that it is *highly improbable* that these four circumstances are necessary or unavoidable? For otherwise, would it be appropriate to speak of the 'utmost license' if someone supposed that they were necessary?

In saying that something is 'necessary or unavoidable', what Philo is saying, presumably, is that it could only be avoided at a cost that would outweigh the benefit of doing so. So something is necessary or unavoidable if and only if its existence is morally justifiable. Accordingly, Philo is claiming that it is very unlikely that the four circumstances in question are ones whose existence is morally justifiable.

It would seem, then, that Hume at the point is advancing what is in effect a probabilistic or evidential version of the argument from evil. For rather than claiming that it is *impossible* that the four features in question are morally justifiable, and hence that they are incompatible with the existence of a good deity who knew of their existence, and had the power to eliminate them, Hume is claiming only that it is *unlikely* that they are morally justifiable, from which it will follow only that it is unlikely that there exists a morally good deity who knows of their existence, and who has the power to eliminate those features.

What are the four features that Philo has in mind? The first is this:

The *first* circumstance which introduces evil is that contrivance or economy of the animal creation by which pains, as well as pleasures, are employed to excite all creatures to action, and make them vigilant in the great work of self – preservation. (1980: 69)

Philo argues that pain is unnecessary, his basic proposal being that animals, rather than being caused by pain to perform actions that contribute to their survival, could be motivated instead by diminution of pleasure.

Whether diminution of pleasure would be effective might well be questioned. But Hume's basic contention here – that pain is unnecessary – seems right. Organisms could become aware of dangers to their bodies via the same nerves as now give rise to experiences of pain, but rather than pain centres in the brain, there could be centres that would produce non-voluntary responses withdrawing the relevant bodily part from the object threatening to damage the body. It would seem, then, that painful sensations are not necessary.

The second feature Philo mentions is that events occur in accordance with exceptionless laws of nature:

> But a capacity of pain would not alone produce pain were it not for the *second* circumstance, viz., the conducting of the world by general laws; and this seems nowise necessary to a very perfect being. It is true, if everything were conducted by particular volitions, the course of nature would be perpetually broken, and no man could employ his reason in the conduct of life. But might not other particular volitions remedy this inconvenience? In short, might not the Deity exterminate all ill, wherever it were to be found, and produce all good, without any preparation or long progress of causes and effects? (1980: 70)

Philo, at this point, seems to overstate how much intervention would be needed. For, in the first place, the events that cause massive suffering and death are relatively rare. Moreover, the type of intervention needed to prevent earthquakes, or tsunamis, or plagues could almost always be completely undetectable. So cases where intervention would be needed of such a sort that people could conclude that a supernatural being must have intervened could be very rare. Hume is mistaken, then, in saying that 'the course of nature would be perpetually broken', and in concluding, thereby, that 'no man could employ his reason in the conduct of life'.

Philo immediately proceeds, however, to reject his initial characterization, and argues, instead, that many events are contrary to our expectations, and that human life depends on many accidents. Because of this (1980: 108), 'A being, therefore, who knows the secret springs of the universe might easily, by particular volitions, turn all these accidents to the good of mankind and render the whole world happy, without discovering himself in any operation.' Consequently,

> A few such events as these, regularly and wisely conducted, would change the face of the world; and yet would no more seem to disturb the course of nature or confound human conduct than the present economy of things, where the causes are secret and variable and compounded. Some small touches given to *Caligula's* brain in his infancy might have converted him into a *Trajan*. One wave, a little higher than the rest, by burying *Caesar* and his fortune in the bottom of the ocean, might have restored liberty to a considerable part of mankind. (1980: 70)

Hume's examples are extremely effective, and show very vividly the extent to which present-day theists, such as Peter van Inwagen in his book *The Problem of Evil* and elsewhere, grossly exaggerate both the amount of intervention that would be needed to radically reduce the suffering in the world, and the extent to which such intervention would be detectable.

The third feature – of which Philo says that, given its absence, much less suffering would arise from the first two features he mentioned – is that organisms have not been at all well equipped with regard to powers that would enable them to avoid much suffering:

> In short, nature seems to have formed an exact calculation of the necessities of her creatures; and, like a *rigid master,* has afforded them little more powers or endowments than what are strictly sufficient to supply those necessities. An *indulgent parent* would have bestowed a large stock in order to guard against accidents, and secure the happiness and welfare of the creature in the most unfortunate concurrence of circumstances. (1980: 110)

The fourth and final feature Philo mentions as contributing greatly to suffering is this:

> The fourth circumstance whence arises the misery and ill of the universe is the inaccurate workmanship of all the springs and principles of the great machine of nature. It must be acknowledged that there are few parts of the universe which seem not to serve some purpose, and whose removal would not produce a visible defect and disorder in the whole, The parts hang all together, nor can one be touched without affecting the rest, in a greater or less degree. But at the same time, it must be observed that none of these parts or principles, however useful, are so accurately adjusted as to keep precisely within those bounds in which their utility consists; but they are, all of them, apt, on every occasion, to run into the one extreme or the other. One would imagine that this grand production had not

received the last hand of the maker; so little finished is every part, and so coarse are the strokes with which it is executed. Thus the winds are requisite to convey the vapors along the surface of the globe, and to assist men in navigation: But how often, rising up to tempests and hurricanes, do they become pernicious? Rains are necessary to nourish all the plants and animals of the earth: But how often are they defective? how often excessive? (1980: 73)

Philo then sums up the situation as follows:

On the concurrence, then, of these four circumstances does all or the greatest part of natural evil depend. Were all living creatures incapable of pain, or were the world administered by particular volitions, evil never could have found access into the universe: And were animals endowed with a large stock of powers and faculties, beyond what strict necessity requires, or were the several springs and principles of the universe so accurately framed as to preserve always the just temperament and medium, there must have been very little ill in comparison of what we feel at present. (1980: 73)

Philo is unwilling to assert that these four features are unnecessary. It is *possible* that the world is a better place for having such features than it would be given their absence. What Philo claims, once again, is simply that unless one has some plausible *a priori* argument for the goodness of a creator, one is not justified, given these very general, and to all appearances, highly undesirable features of the world, in inferring, from the observed phenomena, that there is a very powerful, intelligent and *good* creator:

But let us still assert that, as this goodness is not antecedently established but must be inferred from the phenomena, there can be no grounds for such an inference while there are so many ills in the universe, and while these ills might so easily have been remedied, as far as human understanding can be allowed to judge on such a subject. (1980: 74)

Hume's probabilistic version of the argument from evil

Although we are nearly at the end of Hume's discussion of the problem of evil in Parts X and XI of the *Dialogues*, Philo sets out, at this point, what is, I think, Hume's most important argument. He begins by asking the reader to consider the universe, and suggests that when one does so,

The whole present nothing but the idea of a blind nature, impregnated by a great vivifying principle, and pouring forth from her lap, without discernment or parental care, her maimed and abortive children! (1980: 74)

This description leads to Philo's mentioning 'the Manichaean system', according to which the world is run by both a good being and an evil one, and Philo says that in some respects the Manichaean hypothesis 'has more probability than the common hypothesis, by giving a plausible account of the strange mixture of good and ill which appears in life'. (1980: 74). But he goes on to note that the world does not give the appearance of a battleground of good and evil, which counts against Manichaeanism.

Philo then proceeds to say very explicitly both what he thinks is the correct view of the world, and the ground of his opinion on that matter:

> The true conclusion is that the original source of all things is entirely indifferent to all these principles, and has no more regard to good above ill than to heat above cold, or to drought above moisture, or to light above heavy.
> There may *four* hypotheses be framed concerning the first causes of the universe: *that* they are endowed with perfect goodness; *that* they have perfect malice; *that* they are opposite and have both goodness and malice; *that* they have neither goodness nor malice. Mixed phenomena can never prove the two former unmixed principles; and the uniformity and steadiness of general laws seem to oppose the third. The fourth, therefore, seems by far the most probable. (1980: 75)

Notice that, on the one hand, Philo holds that, in view of the mixed nature of phenomena with regard to good and evil, there is no possibility of proving that either of the first two hypotheses is true. So, once again, Philo is claiming that there is no sound inference to the conclusion that there is a good creator of the world. But here he does not rest with that conclusion. Instead, he immediately goes on to say that fourth hypothesis 'seems by far the most probable'.

But if this is right, then even if one were to assign a probability of zero both to the hypothesis that the first causes of the universe 'have perfect malice' and to the hypothesis that the first causes of the universe 'are opposite and have both goodness and malice', the probability that the first causes of the universe 'are endowed with perfect goodness' would have to have a probability that is *substantially less than one half*.

It seems clear, moreover, that Hume did not think that the second and third hypotheses had much lower probabilities than the first hypothesis. Given the difficulty, to Hume's mind, of judging whether the goodness in the world outbalances the evil in the world, or vice versa, and given that he says that the Manichaean hypothesis is in some respects more probable than the common, theistic hypothesis, it appears that Hume probably viewed the first three hypotheses as rather close with respect to probability. But, if so, then given that the fourth hypothesis is 'by far the most probable', the conclusion is that the belief that there is a good creator must have a probability *substantially less than one quarter*.

The upshot is that, in the end, Philo, and therefore Hume, rather than merely attempting to block an inference to a theistic conclusion, is advancing a version of the inductive argument from evil.

The argument is not, of course, very fully developed. In particular, Philo has not shown that, of the four hypotheses he mentions, the fourth is 'by far the most probable'. But we have the core of a very promising argument, and it is not hard to see how it might be filled out. Thus, leaving aside the Manichean hypothesis, the other three hypotheses have precisely the same logical form, and differ only in whether it is perfect goodness, or perfect malice, or perfect indifference that is ascribed to the first cause or causes of the universe, and given that, it would seem that a sound indifference principle will generate the conclusion that those three hypotheses should be assigned equal *a priori* probabilities. Then one can ask either which hypothesis best explains the observed phenomena, or which hypothesis generates the best predictions. With regard to the former, it surely is not at all plausible that a world where it is hard to tell whether the goodness exceeds the evil or vice versa is better explained either by the hypothesis that the first causes of the universe possess perfect goodness, or by the hypothesis that the first causes of the universe possess perfect malice, rather than by the hypothesis that the first causes of the universe have neither goodness nor malice. Alternatively, if one prefers to approach the issue by focusing upon predictions, then, if the fourth hypothesis is true, there is nothing that makes good states of affairs more likely than bad ones, or vice versa, and so it would seem likely that the world will contain a reasonably balanced mixture of the two, as is the case. By contrast, if the first hypothesis is true, there is reason for expecting good states of affairs to be much more common than bad ones. But this prediction is false. Similarly, if the second hypothesis is true, there is reason for expecting bad states of affairs to be much more common than good ones, and this prediction is also false. Judging by the success or failure of predictions, therefore, the conclusion is that the fourth hypothesis is much more probable than either the first or the second.

The lines of thought just mentioned, moreover, are not novel ones, unrelated to Hume's own thinking. For recall the following claim, advanced by Philo, and discussed above:

> In short, I repeat the question: Is the world, considered in general and as it appears to us in this life, different from what a man or such a limited being would, *beforehand,* expect from a very powerful, wise, and benevolent Deity? It must be strange prejudice to assert the contrary. (1980: 69)

Expectations are predictions, and once Philo's four hypotheses are on the table, and one is considering which of those hypotheses is most likely to be true, then Philo's earlier observation becomes very relevant indeed.

Summing up: Hume's achievements

Philo, speaking for Hume, seems clearly to hold that the existence of evil is logically incompatible with the existence of an omnipotent, omniscient and morally perfect creator. On this matter, most philosophers think, and in my opinion correctly, that Hume was wrong.

Hume's achievements in this area are, nevertheless, extraordinarily impressive. First of all, in discussing the problem of evil, he focused upon the wide variety of terrible evils that are found in the world. In this respect, his approach contrasts sharply with the way in which the problem of evil was discussed for much of the twentieth century, when most philosophers attempted to formulate things in terms of facts such as the mere existence of evil. As noted earlier, it was some time before philosophers realized that such abstract formulations were a mistake.

Second, in Part X of the *Dialogues*, Hume's discussion is concerned with the existence of an infinite deity – a being with unlimited knowledge, power and goodness – but at the beginning of Part XI, the focus shifts to the bearing of evil upon the existence of a finite deity. Hume realized very clearly, then, what many subsequent philosophers failed to, namely, that the existence of evil in the world poses a problem not just for the God of classical monotheism, but for many other deities as well.

Third, this shift is also important because of its implications for the correct logical form of the argument from evil. When one focuses only upon the existence of an omnipotent, omniscient and morally perfect being, it is very natural to think in terms of incompatibility arguments, and to attempt to show that the existence of evil is logically incompatible with the existence of God, whereas when one considers the existence of a deity that is not all-powerful, or all-knowing, or less than perfectly good, then the idea of showing that the mere existence of any evil at all is logically incompatible with the existence of such a being has very little plausibility, and so the discussion naturally shifts to the question of whether there are facts about the evils actually found in the world that render improbable the existence of the finite deity that one is considering. In short, the focus shifts to evidential, or probabilistic, versions of the argument from evil.

Fourth, what the theist would ideally like to do – though I think that most theists, aside from a few philosophers such as John Hick (1966) and Richard Swinburne (1979), have come to feel that the task is more or less hopeless – is to offer a theodicy, understood as an account of reasons that, regardless of whether they are God's actual reasons for allowing various evils in the world, would be morally sufficient reasons for allowing those evils. Philo's concrete and vivid descriptions of the many types of evils found in the world makes it clear to the reader just how daunting the task of offering a theodicy is. But also very important, it seems to me, are Philo's '*four* circumstances on which depend all or the greatest part of the ills that molest sensible creatures' (1980: 69), since Hume is there describing certain features of the world that do not seem at all necessary, and that, if changed, would appear to make for an enormous reduction of evil in the world.

Fifth, before Hume's *Dialogues Concerning Natural Religion* appeared, religious thinkers could naturally think of the intellectual situation in the following terms. On the one hand, there is what Philo refers to as 'the common hypothesis' (1980: 74) – namely, that God exists – and, on the other hand, there is the problem posed by evil, and the task is to fend off the threat posed by the latter. But once the idea of there being a number of competing hypothesis is thrust to the centre of the stage – as it is with Philo's remark, 'There may *four* hypotheses be framed concerning the first causes of the universe' (1980: 75) – everything is changed, for now the question that *should* be addressed, though usually it is not, is which of those competing hypotheses is most likely to be true.

Finally, and perhaps most important of all, when that question is asked, it may very well turn out, as Philo claims, that the hypothesis that is 'by far the most probable' is that the first causes of the universe 'have neither goodness nor malice' (1980: 75). The upshot, as we have seen, is that Hume is, in the end, advancing a probabilistic version of the argument from evil, and one which, though not at all fully developed, seems very promising indeed.

Notes

1 Milton: *Paradise Lost*, XI.
2 One might also think that the following hypothesis was equally likely: 'E: The cause or causes of the world are evil.' However the latter hypothesis is not relevant to the present argument.

Bibliography

Alvin Plantinga. (1979) 'The Probabilistic Argument from Evil', *Philosophical Studies* 35, 1–53.

David Hume. (1959) *Dialogues Concerning Natural Religion*, ed. David Aiken. New York: Hafner Publishing Company.

David Hume. (1779) *Dialogues Concerning Natural Religion*.

David Hume. (1980). *Dialogues Concerning Natural Religion*, ed. Richard H. Popkin. Indianapolis, Indiana: Hackett Publishing Company.

David Hume. (1993) *Dialogues Concerning Natural Religion*, and *The Natural History of Religion*, (ed.) J. C. A. Gaskin. Oxford and New York: Oxford University Press.

David O'Connor. (2001) *Hume on Religion*. London: Routledge.

Gaskin, J. C. A. (1978) *Hume's Philosophy of Religion*. London and Basingstoke: Macmillan.

James Noxon. (1964) 'Hume's Agnosticism', *The Philosophical Review* 73/2, 248–61. Reprinted in *Hume: A Collection of Critical Essay,* (ed.) V. C. Chappell, Garden City, New York: Doubleday, 1966, 361–83.

John Hick. (1966) *Evil and the God of Love*. New York: Harper and Row.

Michael Tooley and Alvin Plantinga. (2008) *Knowledge of God*. Oxford: Blackwell Publishing.

Nelson Pike. (1963) 'Hume on Evil', *The Philosophical Review* 72/2, 180–97.

Norman Kemp Smith. (1935) Introduction to David Hume's *Dialogues Concerning Natural Religion*, (ed.) Norman Kemp Smith. Oxford and New York: Oxford University Press.

Peter van Inwagen. (2008) *The Problem of Evil*. New York: Oxford University Press.

Richard Swinburne. (1979) *The Existence of God*. Oxford: Clarendon Press.

Stewart M. A. (1994) 'An Early Fragment on Evil', in *Hume and Hume's Connexions*, (ed.) M. A. Stewart and John P. Wright, University Park, Pennsylvania, The Pennsylvania State University Press, 160–70. (Stewart's article contains a photocopy of Hume's manuscript.)

William Rowe. (1979) 'The Problem of Evil and Some Varieties of Atheism', *American Philosophical Quarterly* 16, 335–41.

SUGGESTIONS FOR FURTHER READING

Two classic works in the field of philosophy of religion are David Hume's posthumously published *Dialogues Concerning Natural Religion* (1779); and William James's 1904 *The Varieties of Religious Experience*. Among books that survey the traditional theistic arguments, Stephen T. Davis' *God, Reason & Theistic Proofs* (Eerdmans Publishing Co., 1997) is a readable survey by a theist of the various theistic arguments examined in this book. J.L. Mackie's *The Miracle of Theism* (Oxford University Press, 1982) provides a critical review of the traditional theistic arguments, and a chapter on the problem of evil.

Chapter 2: Open theism is introduced in *The Openness of God: A biblical challenge to the traditional understanding of God*, ed. C. Pennock (Intervarsity Press, 1995), and is argued for in *The God Who Risks: A theology of providence* (Intervarsity Press, 1998) by John Sanders. It is critiqued in Bruce Ware's *Their God is too Small* (Crossway, 2003). See also the book, *Perspectives on the Doctrine of God: 4 views* (B&H Academic, 2008) which presents a debate concerning four models of the nature of God.

Chapter 3: the best overview of the ontological argument is Graham Oppy's *Ontological Arguments and Belief in God* (Cambridge University Press, 1996). A short and sympathetic introduction to the ontological argument can be found in Alvin Plantinga's *God, Freedom and Evil* (Eerdman's Publishing Co., 1980). Many of the historically important texts concerning the ontological argument are collected in *The Ontological Argument*, ed. Alvin Plantinga (Anchor Books, 1965). A popular treatment of the argument is found in Larry Witham's *The Proof of God* (Atlas & Co., 2008).

Chapter 4: a thorough review of Thomas Aquinas's five ways of proving God's existence is found in Anthony Kenny's *The Five ways: St. Thomas' Proofs of God's Existence* (University of Notre Dame Press, 1980). William Rowe's *The Cosmological Argument* (Fordham University Press, 1998) is a fine examination of Samuel Clarke's eighteen century version of the cosmological argument. William Lane Craig examines *The Kalām Cosmological Argument* (MacMillan Press, 1979).

Chapter 5: a wonderful collection of essays on the current state of the design argument is *God and Design: The teleological argument and modern science*, ed. N. A. Manson (Routledge, 2003). A short and readable general introduction to the design argument is The Argument from Design, by Thomas McPherson (MacMillian, 1972). John Leslie's Universes (Routledge, 1989) should be read by any with an interest in the design argument.

Chapter 6: Two books examining Kant's thoughts on the philosophy of religion include Allen Wood's *Kant's Rational Theology* (Cornell University Press, 1978) which looks at Kant's critique of the three traditional arguments and his thoughts on the idea of God; and Peter Byrne's *Kant on God* (Ashgate, 2007), which examines a broader range of topics, including Kant's positive case for God. An examination of moral arguments generally can be found in William Wainwright's *Religion and Morality* (Ashgate, 2005).

Chapter 7: Richard Gale's *The Philosophy of William James: An introduction* (Cambridge University Press, 2005) provides an overview of James the philosopher. William Alston's *Perceiving God: An epistemology of religious experience* (Cornell University Press, 1991) is an important contemporary work examining the philosophical significance of religious experience.

Chapter 8: A general overview and critique of the wager is found in Jeff Jordan, *Pascal's Wager: Pragmatic arguments and belief in God* (Oxford University Press, 2006). Pascal's life and work, in addition to the wager, is surveyed in James A. Connor, *Pascal's Wager: The man who played dice with God* (Harper, 2006).

Chapter 9: An accessible general introduction to the philosophical problem of miracles is found in Richard Swinburne's *The Concept of Miracle* (St. Martin's Press, 1970). The historical context of Hume's essay on miracles is explored in R. M. Burns, *The Great Debate on Miracles: From Joseph Glanvill to David Hume* (Bucknell University Press, 1981).

Chapter 10: Two fine collections of classic and contemporary readings on the problem of evil are *The Problem of Evil*, ed. M. McCord Adams & R. M. Adams (Oxford University Press, 1990), and *God and the Problem of Evil*, ed. W. L. Rowe (Basil Blackwell Press, 2001). Two book length studies of David Hume's work in the philosophy of religion are J. C. A. Gaskin, *Hume's Philosophy of Religion* (Humanities Press International, 1988, 2nd edition); and Keith Yandell, *Hume's 'inexpliciable Mystery': His views on religion* (Temple University Press, 1990).

INDEX